THE
CRISIS
AND CHALLENGES
OF BLACK AMERICA

BY TYRONE AND DEBRA HUGHES

BALBOA.PRESS

A DIVISION OF HAY HOUSE

Balboa Press books may be ordered through booksellers or by contacting:

Balboa Press
A Division of Hay House
1663 Liberty Drive
Bloomington, IN 47403
www.balboapress.com
844-682-1282

Because of the dynamic nature of the Internet, any web addresses or links contained in this book may have changed since publication and may no longer be valid. The views expressed in this work are solely those of the author and do not necessarily reflect the views of the publisher, and the publisher hereby disclaims any responsibility for them.

The author of this book does not dispense medical advice or prescribe the use of any technique as a form of treatment for physical, emotional, or medical problems without the advice of a physician, either directly or indirectly. The intent of the author is only to offer information of a general nature to help you in your quest for emotional and spiritual well-being. In the event you use any of the information in this book for yourself, which is your constitutional right, the author and the publisher assume no responsibility for your actions.

Any people depicted in stock imagery provided by Getty Images are models, and such images are being used for illustrative purposes only.
Certain stock imagery © Getty Images.

All Scriptures taken from the KJV version of the bible.

Print information available on the last page.

ISBN: 978-1-9822-7186-2 (sc)
ISBN: 978-1-9822-7187-9 (e)

Balboa Press rev. date: 07/22/2021

CONTENTS

OPENING THOUGHT

Why is this narrative important, and why was it written? Can I utter words that hasn't been expressed, or articulate what historians and theologians have not said as it pertains to black folks?

My reason for writing the Crisis and Challenges of Black America is in hope of giving birth to the fresh need of solidarity and unity within our regal and great culture. I believe that history has defined us wrongly, unjustly, and in words of unrighteousness. I am writing this narrative with the divine purpose and hope of liberating my people from self- destruction, and from the global vices that destroy who we are as a royal diadem of God. We cannot use 1950 answers for 2021 questions.

It is my intent to open our eyes with today's truth of our struggles, and to reveal the truth about our collective blackness. I write from the perspective of the blessed, marginalized, of the oppressed, and of the disregarded. However, I do not put pen to paper with an attitude of weakness, passivity, meritocracy of suffering, or in terms of redemptive pain.

I will hopefully bring to the table of established intellectuals, the unlearned, the un-churched, and the anointed, the same message of a need to speak up for who we really are, and to speak out against both who we are not and against the horrors that continue to plague our growth and development as a divine people birthed from the image and likeness of God.

The Crisis and Challenges of Black America are not defined by any class of people due to location, spiritual beliefs, dogma, doctrine, or pedigree.

I am writing this social narrative of what we are facing in a global pandemic, a political upheaval, social unrest, mass incarceration, unparalleled drug addictions, sexual revolutions of untold proportions, a depressing economy, Church divide, and broken humanity.

In this text I use many sources of great thinkers with a plethora of beliefs that I believe will underscore the thought and theme of this grand narrative which Is composed trough existential, spiritual, social, and educational truth. Our Liberating Lord can truly elevate a species that is in danger of being destroyed. Within this literary articulation of the crisis and challenges of black America, I use many Biblical text, not to exclude the beliefs of others, but to confirm a need for the teachings of Jesus to encompass our lives and thought process. Regardless of what we believe or disbelieve, who can disagree that we need forgiveness, mercy, grace, love, healing, life and life more abundantly, Financial provision, and salvation or the mending of the soul and spirit of man?

The persona of Christ is symbolic of those redeeming qualities that I feel we must emulate if we are to achieve our greatness as a people. And so... I write this narrative not because I have all the answers for the feminist, gay, agnostic, atheist, non-Christian, Christian, secular humanist, economist, or the scientist. however, I pose the answers to who we are, and what we can achieve through unity, solidarity, patriotic loyalty of black nationalism, Afrocentricity, negritude, and global love for one another in spite of our differences.

It is not my purpose to bend your beliefs nor for you to agree with me. I am simply a mirror. Look into it, and if you like what you see, simply love being you and move on with life and live it to the full. However, as you get naked. Every pound, wrinkle, cellulite, gray hair, dent, scar, and pimple will be seen. If you want change, for that reason, I wrote this narrative. For too long we have asked to be brought to the table of other cultures, to be accepted by others, when we were created in the image and likeness of

God. As a nation of people, I believe we should be striving to emulate Jesus, to reflect who god created us to be in both love and character.

I hope you enjoy this journey.

I would like to thank my beautiful wife minister Debra Hughes, and all those who influence my life in her immediate family. Giselle, Kim, roger, Ricky, Lanita, Rose Marie, Kristen, Pastor Hillis Jeffries, apostle Michael Scott, my mother Mary Beulah Hughes, Blanche Floyd, my family members of the true light army, and my princess and daughter Shantell Hughes my legacy and love.

INTRODUCTION

2020 is a tragic year for families, businesses, churches, and individuals. If I were a betting man, I do not think I would be alone by saying I will be glad when this year is over. With that said, what will the new year bring? If you are like me, you have heard enough of so-called "prophecies." I can recall how this unforgettable year began with powerful declarations proclaiming that this was the year of perfect vision. I heard that people would gain victory in their lives like never before, and how this magical year would bring prosperity, with the church excelling in personal healing and soul winning like no other time in human history.

However, I never heard one prophet, who claim to have the ears of God, say that 2020 would bring a plague that would torture children, maim elderly people, cripple our economy, strangle us in corrupt politics, and eliminate over a million people worldwide in a sudden death sentence. While listening to these world renown apostles and prophets, I never heard that churches would close and would leave thousands to wonder where can they turn if not to the church of Christ? We are living in dark and perilous times.

Sadly enough, I have heard about too many people dying from the deadly Corona Virus. No nation, kindred, creed, or language has gone untouched and unaffected by this global pandemic.

Even the rich felt the pinch as millions of jobs were considered non-essential, and the economy crashed like a drunken driver. Over 51 million people became suddenly unemployed. People across the globe lost their homes to foreclosure, cars were repossessed, schools were closed, race riots erupted across America, police officers maliciously gunned down unarmed citizens without legal ramifications.

In the year 2020, we saw record numbers of suicide, and drug overdoses among our youth. Unfortunately, we saw natural disasters wreak havoc upon this country, in addition to the fall of an American president with record numbers turning out to vote for change in the white house.

So where do we go from here? A lot has happened to give birth to doubt inside the minds of many people across the world. I do not think I would be wrong to ask this question. Have we lost faith with God being in control over both our lives and over the world?

If we still believe, then are we challenged with why has He allowed such tragedy and chaos to touch the lives of so many of His children?

I will be the first person to tell you that I do not have all the answers to the plethora of questions asked by the people. However, I can offer you the word of God that will hopefully open your eyes to the many blessings that are available even in the tragedy of a global pandemic.

If you are anything like me, you could use some good news. I am tired of doom and gloom news, Corona fatalities, funerals, sick and shut in announcements on the church call line, and yet another political scandal or a cheating pastor from a mega-church.

Let us face it. We need help as a nation. We need healing, racial reconciliation, economic restoration beyond a stimulus package, fresh leadership, clarity of vision, moral direction, and open hearts that are receptive to love and unity. I guess it is easier said than done, right?

Is There anything too hard for God?

Think about this for a moment. We know that humanity could not have created the universe. As human beings, we cannot breathe without air, or oxygen. Therefore, the earth had to have been here before man. What type of intelligence does it take to create an estimated 100 billion galaxies? Or 8.7 million species of animals?

What type of power does it take to watch over and be responsible for 7.594 billion people upon the earth? Can man do any of this?

Absolutely not. Therefore, I passionately believe that God is in control. Even though millions have been touched by this epic pandemic. I have been among the blessed and fortunate. Yes, I have loss jobs and have been denied work. However, God has always supported both my wife and I, in addition to my immediate family throughout this crisis. My wife and I took a vow before God. We simply said, we are not going to get sick from the Corona Virus! We stand firm upon the word of God and we walk daily by faith and cancel out any thoughts or suggestions that we live in fear over what the Lord has given us dominion over.

<u>What am I believing God for?</u>

"Then He called His disciples together, and gave them power and authority over all devils, and to cure diseases." (Luke 9: 1)

"Never allow the importance of your decisions to outweigh the consequences."

Every decision that I make will affect someone who is connected to my life. Bad choices carry detrimental results. Wise decisions will reap positive fruit.

The world that we live in needs answers and I passionately believe that within these pages you will become enlightened and blessed beyond measure. I will not promise you a pie in the sky, a million dollars over night, instant success, or the best spouse ever created. What I will promise you is the truth of the gospel.

If you take to heart and apply the sacred word of God to your lives, you will achieve everything that God has promised you from the bedroom to the bank account.

CHAPTER ONE

RELATIONSHIPS

"And the Lord God formed man of the dust of the ground and breathed into his nostrils the breath of life; and man became a living soul." (Genesis 2: 7)

"Even everyone who is called by my name, whom I created for my glory, whom I formed and made." (Isaiah 43: 7)

One of the reasons why I believe Satan released this deadly plague upon the earth was to destroy the bond of relationships. Corona has created a universal fear of the human touch, and the closeness of people. Yet, we see from the above verses that God created us with His hands.

Therefore, we are created to respond to touch. The word of the Lord tells us that God is love. (1 John 4:8)

As we unfold this truth, we will discover that not only are we meant to respond to touch, but we are to expect that touch to be one of love. In the absence of human closeness, and caring embraces, we become a nation of people who are trying to live outside of why and how we were created by God. "The thief comes only to steal and kill and destroy; I (Jesus) have come that they (whom Satan attacks) may have life and have it to the full." (John 10: 10)

As we look at events unfold across this nation. We can clearly see the problem of broken relationships. Sociology teaches us the vital importance of the interaction between people, and the vast necessity of communication. When we evaluate (Genesis 2:18) "It is not good that man should live alone." Our eyes should open to the purpose of God and His creation. We were given birth by God to have loving relationships, in marriage, fellowship, friendship, and in family unity.

Jesus said, "You will know my disciples (students, followers, or those who believe in my philosophy) if they love one another" (John 13: 34)

Racial tension, police brutality, persecuted churches, sexism, crime, sex trafficking, terrorism, and gang violence are all examples of hatred for one another, which shows us that as a nation we have failed in being the discipled by Jesus.

I understand that many people are against organized religion: big fancy churches, rich pastors, and a group of holier than thou people telling them how to live their lives when they certainly have issues themselves.

However, Jesus is not about a religion. Jesus is the living witness of love, grace, mercy, forgiveness, truth, equality, provision, and compassion. Jesus offers us intimacy through a relationship with our heart, mind, spirit, and soul. He wishes to identify with what is occurring within us. "Cast all your anxiety on Him (Jesus) because He cares for you." (1 Peter 5: 7)

God created man with an individualized touch. He walked and talked with our ancestors Adam and Eve. When Adam disobeyed our Lord and chose a different path other than the loving direction of our heavenly Father, his intimate relationship with God was gravely affected. We were never meant to live at odds with the Lord.

Think about this for a moment. We all have or have had earthly parents. Do you believe you were born to be at war with your parents? Do you think you were born to fight with, oppose, disobey, hate, or challenge those who gave you life? Are you supposed to be afraid of your parents? Examine your childhood.

Truly we can understand that a broken relationship with our parents will affect how we engage in other relationships. We learn how to love and how to treat others from home. Therefore, doesn't it make sense that we learn how to love others by how God loves us?

Let's unpack the following scripture. "And he said, I heard the sound of you in the garden, and I was afraid, because I was naked, and I hid myself." (Genesis 3: 10)

Adam lost his faith in God. In sin he adapted a preconceived notion of thinking that his heavenly Father was looking to punish him, when God was coming to restore him to the loving relationship that they enjoyed before disobedience. With a heart of love God supplied the covering for both His children. * See (Genesis 3: 21; 4: 4)

God understands that if Adam is not restored to the source of love that the Lord stands for, that he would not be able to effectively love his wife Eve, nor his future children.

"Our relationship with God should translate to every relationship that we have with other's"

America and abroad is suffering from being disconnected from the source of love that intimately created us.

The hatred that we see daily within our communities is a direct result of rejecting the only power that can restore our humanity and mend the broken hearts of millions. "Apart from Him (Jesus) we can do nothing." (John 15:5)

Understanding Intimacy

According to therapist Alyssa Mancao, LCSW, "any relationship (romantic or otherwise) requires a combination of all four types of intimacy: emotional, mental, spiritual, and physical." Webster's defines intimacy as a close familiarity or the intimacy between a husband and wife. God wishes to have a personal relationship with us.

"The gospel of Jesus is not a rational concept to be explained in a theory of salvation, but a story about God's presence in Jesus' solidarity with the oppressed, which led to His death on the cross. What is redemptive is the faith that God snatches victory out of defeat, life out of death, and hope out of despair." (James H, Cone, the Cross and the Lynching Tree, 2013).

There are three imperative places in the Bible that teaches us that the will of God is intimacy with His children.

- ➢ Genesis 3:9 And the Lord God called unto Adam
- ➢ Exodus 25: 22 And I will meet with you there above the mercy seat
- ➢ John 15:26 But when the Comforter is come, whom I will send unto you from the Father

The Economy of God by Witness Lee, 1968 states: "The residence of God is our human spirit. For us believers, God is not a faraway, objective God; He exists in us to be in our life forever."

If we wish to learn of God's intimacy with His children, we need look no further than Abraham the father of faith, and Moses the great liberator.

"I will bless you and make you famous, and you will be a blessing to others." (Genesis 22: 2)

"And through your offspring all nations of the earth will be blessed, because you have obeyed me." (Genesis 22: 18)

God spoke to Abraham, He led Abraham to a place of fruitfulness in both land, body, materialism, and spiritually. In appreciation, Abraham was the first person in the Bible to tithe, which revealed to us the importance of sowing into the kingdom of our Lord and Savior. Investing in the spiritual things of God, supports our earthly needs. We can learn this invaluable lesson through Abraham giving to the priesthood of Melchizedek as depicted in (Genesis 14:20)

Melchizedek is a type of Christ through a priesthood which has no origin of earth.

His priestly office was not an appointment from man, His sovereign rule shall never end, it will not cease with the death of an earthly priest.

Abraham's tithe given to the preincarnate Christ blessed his future grandchildren. What we do in the spirit affects what happens in the earth.

"In addition, we might even say that these Levites the ones who collect the tithe paid a tithe to Melchizedek when their ancestor Abraham paid a tithe to him." (Hebrew7:9) New Living Translation.

A testament to who we are is our faith in Christ through the application of our devoted lives to Him. God constantly displayed an intimate relationship with Abraham. God opened the womb of his wife Sarah. He wanted His spiritual son to be blessed with children from the woman that he loved. He gave wealth to Abraham which allowed him to bless people in the earth and to leave a legacy to his sons Isaac and Jacob. God showed us the trust level that we can enjoy in His provision, even when He may ask of us a challenging thing.

Then God said, "Take your son, your only son, whom you love Isaac and go to the region of Moriah. Sacrifice him there as a burnt offering on the mountain I will show you." (Genesis 22: 2) We see the intimate trust in God's provision through Abraham's willingness to sacrifice his son that he loved. Thus, we also see that the Lord's response to Abraham's trust is provision, through His supplying a sacrifice for him in the end.

In Christ we will always gain the victory, as illustrated in this powerful promise. "Many are the afflictions of the righteous, but they are delivered from them all." (Psalm 34:19)

Through the relationship that Moses had with God a nation of people was delivered from bondage. The children of Israel were shown the Lord's acts, but to Moses He showed him His ways which allowed him the ability to lead as God leads. (Psalm 103: 7)

CHAPTER TWO

LET THERE BE LIGHT

Devon stood looking out the window of his shack for an apartment. He was tired of living in squalor while everyone else drove around in nice cars, ate in five-star restaurants, dressed in designer clothes, slept with the best of women, and lived in spacious houses or condominiums. Well, today his fortune would change one way or the other. Devon deeply believed that America and its systemic racism will never give a black man a decent chance to receive help from the spoils of the great American dream.

In the hearts of many, this country only rewards black men for entertaining whites through comedy, or through the venue of sports, and movies.

"Well," thought the embittered black man from the ghettoes of Chicago. "That changes today!" In this generation, Chicago is better known to the world as Chiraq. Chiraq became the nickname of Chicago due to the massive amount of murders in the urban community, which is particularly among the black youth, through drugs, gangs, and crime. Chicago is reminiscent of the war-torn Iraq. Devon looked over at the table where the poignant book he had just read about his hero Malcolm X lay. "The Roosting Chickens." He agreed with brother Malcolm when he articulated that when John F. Kennedy was assassinated in 1963 that it was "merely a case of chickens coming home to roost"

America must pay. Devon picked up his cell phone. Yes, time to use the horrid conditions of COVID-19 to his advantage. Twenty-five minutes later, Devon and his best friend Rico moved swiftly into a white owned pawn shop over on the cities north side. Who could ever name them? Who cares about cameras? He should have been thought of this. The world was asked to wear mask, and gloves for sanitation reasons.

Well…why not use this opportunity to get money through robbing these rich white folks who hold minorities down anyway? That brother Malcolm X was a genius.

Before the unsuspecting store owner knew what was happening, he had a nine-millimeter pointed at his head. "Don't move!"

The two young black men raced away from the scene of the crime laughing at the fear that they had caused, and the money they had stolen. Devon began bragging to his protégé.

"We can get rich doing this. And think about it. This is the perfect time too."

"Why you say that?" Rico asked.

"Man, after the cops killed George Floyd, and that black girl in her apartment, the police are leery about running up on us. Plus, I figure if they do, we can just make a loud scene and if they shoot us, at least our families will get millions of dollars from the city. Heck, that is one way to get out from under the roach and rat-infested dilapidated housing of Chicago."

Wow! Rico thought. "I never thought of it like that. We can make our lives count for something now. And if we die in the process, at least our poor mom and pops will be straight for the rest of their lives."

"Yeah my man." Devon said. "Now let's call up a couple of chicks, get a fancy hotel room and celebrate like the rich folks for a change." Rico loved the sound of that. Living good from the bedroom to the bank account.

I grew up much like Devon and Rico, in the rough and tough streets of Detroit, Michigan, on the west side of town over by Grand River and Green field. My hood was notorious for gangs. We did not have the Bloods, Crips, Gangster Disciples, or the Vice Lords like today's youth.

Detroit was infected by over twenty-five dangerous gangs like the Earl Flynn's, The Latin Kings, The Chain Gang, Black killers, the Money Makers, and most of all the deadly Young Boy Incorporated.

The schools I attended were hardcore. At the age of fifteen most of my friends carried pistols to school. Gang violence was a major problem all over the city. Drug dealers covered every corner. If you wanted to wear nice clothes and Jordan's to school, you better be ready to fight to keep them. Even though I was raised in a Christian home, I did not want to hear that church mumbo-jumbo.

I was young gifted and black. I was about getting that money! The mentality in the hood was this. America was not going to give us city boys nothing!

Therefore, we had to get out there and take what we wanted. We shot first and asked questions later. If you wanted the pretty girls that put out (had sex) you had to have a car, money, a place to take them, and nice clothes. Everything that my Mom taught my siblings, and I was different than what the streets indoctrinated into our minds.

Sex out of wedlock is fornication and wrong in the Bible. But to us if both people said yes, hey, it is all good. Drinking and smoking in the Bible is defiling the temple, which is your body, to us however, it felt good and made life easier to cope with.

It didn't take long before I had been shot, stabbed, addicted to drugs, and sentenced to the penitentiary where I would end up serving twenty-seven years in maximum security prisons in four different states. Ohio, Kansas, Kentucky, and Alabama.

"Darkness cannot drive out darkness; only light can do that. Hate cannot drive out hate; only love can do that"

Martin Luther King Jr.

One day while looking in the mirror during a very dark moment in my life. A small voice within me posed a serious question. This was during a season when the terminology keeping it "Real" was popular. The voice taunted me. "What's real about you?" I will never forget this crossroads in my life.

I was thirty years of age. Accusation after accusation seemed to echo and reverberate throughout my psyche..." What's real about you?" Liar, manipulator, con artist, thief, killer, adulterer, robber, drug addict, porn watcher, child of disobedience, prisoner. Tears slowly began to creep down my face. I was nothing. I had failed at being a man, a husband, a father, a student, and a lawful citizen. Everything that my mom raised me to be I was the direct opposite. Most problems that existed within the world, I helped to create. In the year of 1995, I picked up the Bible for myself this time. Not because momma told me to. Not to impress people in prison. Not to try and manipulate God into sending me home early. And not to use it as an emotional crutch to cope with life. I really understood for the first time in my life the meaning of let there be light.

The Lord was saying to me four things.

➤ Let there be a self-awakening of who you are
➤ Let there be an understanding of who I am to you
➤ Let my ways illuminate your life and guide you
➤ Let the mind of Christ also be in you

CHAPTER THREE

"What good is it for someone to gain the entire world, yet forfeit their soul?" (Mark 8:36)

The above text allows us to know that a person can be financially prosperous and not be blessed by God. Judas walked with Christ but stole from him to acquire earthly riches. There are those in the pulpit stealing from God to gain riches.

They are stealing gifts from the church. They are hiring singers to increase church memberships and tithes, and by bringing in talented but unsaved inspirational speakers to feed the flesh of unseasoned church goers. Like Judas, many people are in the proximity of God without being in the presence of the Lord.

The Bible tells us in 2 Timothy that, "For the time will come when they will not endure sound doctrine; but after their own lusts shall they heap to themselves teachers, having itching ears; and they shall turn from the truth, and shall be turned unto fables."

America a nation that once claimed to be up under the mighty banner of "In God We Trust," has changed. We boasted of a democracy that was covered by the blessings of being allies with Israel and anointed by being,

"One Nation Under God." Yet today, we are a capitalist nation that has forsaken God and has pursued the riches of the world.

As an aggregate nation, we are trying to get the blessings of God without being intimate in a holy matrimony with the Bridegroom Jesus.

In our disconnectedness from God we have fallen into a state of intellectual darkness. We believe that we are blessed due to what institution we matriculated from. We are stealing God's glory by promising people things that God never told them is from Him.

We are protesting for every known desire of the flesh. We are at war to live contrary to the word of God. We are striving to gain the world (the promises of Satan) and we are losing the soul of our children, our nation, our marriages, and of our churches. Why? Disobedience.

Let's examine the prayer of the Lord found in John 17:21

"That all of them may be one, Father, just as you are in me and I am in you. May they also be in us so that the world may believe that you have sent me."

Our problem is a broken marriage with the Lord. The election of 2020 was a historical moment in time. Joseph Biden and Kamala Harris earned more votes than any president elect in our history. History was also made as multiple transsexuals were elected to office. In our last election same sex unions were made legal, abortions were made legal.

And so, the problem that we are experiencing is clear. Our Lord and Savior prayed that the two become one, and that we acknowledge that we are neither Jew nor Gentile, male or female, free nor slave.

Our warfare is not carnal. We are in a war with spiritual darkness. We are at war with individualism that rejects the marriage of the Lamb and accepts the vices of the world. Even at the expense of their soul. Yet, there is a sacred solution. I was given this story in a vision.

CHAPTER FOUR

THE TWO SHALL BECOME ONE

O- hear, O heavens, and give ear, O earth, for the Lord hath spoken. I have nourished and brought up children, and they have rebelled against me. Man child, why did you forsake such royalty and sovereign dominion? I gave you matchless wisdom, and a land of gold littered with the finest of jewels in the earth. I blessed you and empowered you to prosper. You were not designed to be a beggar, nor were you formed in weakness or cowardice.

Man-child, you failed in your stewardship of heavenly treasures. My earthly son, why didn't you value what is beyond price? You dined in a flawless garden amidst the tree of life. Every herb yielding tree was your health and enjoyment. I gave you the gift of life, of love, and a most beautiful helper suitable for your every desire. Yet, you listened to a voice contrary to the untold blessings I have bestowed upon you.

The extremely deceptive voice of the world, rich with instant promises led you to crime, and disgrace.

Why man-child did you give up eternal blessings for temporal satisfaction of the flesh? What makes you a man in the world? What are you responsible for? How do you feel after allowing your family to be evicted from their home in my presence within the garden?

What type of man lives the life that is contrary to why you were created? Does the world consider you a man even when you run from commitment, leadership, and fatherhood?

Who are you now O fallen man-child? Who are you faithful to when you are promiscuous in all your ways? Have you no integrity or character? How do you allow someone who does not love you to lie and deceive you with promises of wealth and power when the earth and the fullness thereof belongs to me? Apart from me you are fruitless.

I am silent towards you son of disobedience. Yet, those with an ear shall harken unto my voice. Holy, holy, holy is the Lord of host. The whole earth is full of my glory. Are you listening child? I shed my blood as a dowry for my bride to the Father. You are symbolic of my bride. You were created to be intimate with me to give birth to the plan of my Father.

The man-child tossed and turned in his bed. He fought to break free from this vivid dream that spoke of his reality with such conviction and piercing truth. The voice echoed in his soul…A man does not marry a woman without first having a home for her and the children they will have one day. You lay with women from place to place.

Don't you know that I have prepared a place for my bride? A place of love and eternity. A place of safety, peace, security, and provision.

O man-child let not your heart be troubled; ye say you believe in God, then also believe in me. In my Father's house are many mansions, I will come again for you. Why do you forsake such a great salvation? O wretched man, who can save you? The man-child saw a vision of Jesus sitting high upon a throne, high and lifted up. He started to walk towards him. The majestic beauty and light which looked like the most beautiful rainbow surrounded the throne of grace. He was closer, closer, and suddenly, out of nowhere came another voice and vision. He was able to see all the things that he loved in life. The things that brought him such pleasure. His soul seemed to speak inside his head.

Women of all nationalities danced before his eyes, champagne glasses sparkled in allure, Los Vegas slot machines chimed that winning sound, the fresh aroma of marijuana loomed large in the air. O how can I resist you, when you are so full of pleasure and inviting temptations?

Just the thought of you, the nostalgic aroma of your sweetness captivates me. You heighten my senses with such dazzling ways of promise. Yet, you are a danger, you slowly slither into my emotional crevices and wreak havoc upon my need to feel alive and wanted.

You promise me so much; your scandalous attractions are deadly to morality. Why can't I walk away from you? Your wicked truth disrupts lives through your chameleon style of physical beauty.

Subtly, you squeeze away the breath of righteousness, wrapping your tentacles around the erotic impulses of the flesh. In my selfish quest to be pleased you always trap me with your fangs of lust, and then the poisonous bite of your seduction goes unnoticed because I'm fulfilled with money, party favors, women, and more promises. You taunt me about the rules of heaven, how they will take away what I enjoy, and I will be left like a robot living someone else's dream of greatness and not my own need to be happy on my terms.

The man-child looked into the eyes of sated need that matched his own. Women called out to him, his body shivered in sweet anticipation of ecstasy, quivering, shaking, trembling, and convulsing. Quickly he fell far away from the throne of grace. Unbeknownst, he had entered unto a path of life that leads to disease, violence, poverty, and spiritual death.

The spiritual pull was incredible. His soul yearned for both promises. Which is right? Or is what he craves right, but he is going about achieving it wrong?

The man-child was suddenly enshrouded by light and clarity flashed across his mind and he saw the enemy for who he really is.

O how you have arrested many within their nocturnal addiction, controlling them through your intoxicating persuasions of hedonism, and their own greedy sickness to be had by anyone who will deliver the promises of extreme pleasure. You attract us with gorgeous strangers, with beauty for hire, another's spouse, or even those of the same gender. Your skilled seduction through chat rooms, facetime, zoom meetings, web cam models, and phone chat rooms has beguiled this generation with the exotic feeling of absolute bliss, offered in instant gratification.

Yet, this same overwhelming sensation that warmly caresses the body, and gently embraces the soul, is a powerful elixir that expresses love in a demonstrative way of more than words could ever express. This absolute longing, this undeniable urge to share, to give, and to belong is the ultimate need to be fully immersed in indescribable passions that expresses the sacred beauty of love in the making.

O who can deny when two yearning hearts collide in exotic attraction having purely and happily surrendered one to another in the divine vows of holy matrimony? This consummation of spiritual oneness is lacking nothing in completeness, this magnificent joining is maturation in what God has united. The pleasure is as beautiful as its heavenly purpose, which is to be expressed and enjoyed for a lifetime as the two become one. Yet, serpent. You slither to pervert what is divine and sacred.

You offer unashamed exploitations of the flesh with adult playthings and multiple lovers filled with the poison of fornication.

Your voice echoes from the portals of time. You shall not die. You shall be gods; you will become wise to the secret pleasures that is being kept from you. Even in the face of truth, the man-child struggles to break free from this satanic pull on his soul and spirit.

"He that calls on the name of the Lord shall be saved"
(Acts 2:21)

Help me escapes his trembling lips. The vision of the throne of grace reemerges, and the powerful voice from the heavenlies ring out once again.

"The enemy comes to steal your values, kill who you are spiritually, and to destroy your character and life. Beware, his voice may seem as that of a praise angel, enticing and soothing. He may appear as an angel of light, or he will come as the answer to your prayers. Be not deceived!"

The man-child woke up.

Many of us are faced with problematic decisions on a daily basis. Often, we find ourselves wondering what the big deal about certain things are. However, where we are in life is a direct result of the choices we have made. Salvation is a choice. Eternal damnation is a choice.

Jesus said we will be judged by the words that we speak. I do not think there is a day that goes by whereas there is no temptation of the flesh in one way or another.

I will be the first to admit that I wrestle with not falling back into old behaviors. Yet, I understand that the key to victory is surrendering to become one with God in the spirit. I must decrease so He can increase.

I cannot allow myself to get caught up in someone else's religion or denominational practices that may not line up with the gospel of Jesus Christ. I know that I must keep a personal relationship with my Lord and Savior. I am so thankful that His mercy is new every day, and that His grace is sufficient for my life. I am so blessed just to accept and know that God's love for me is unconditional, and His faith will last forever.

CHAPTER FIVE

"Then was Jesus led up of the spirit into the wilderness to be tested of the devil" (Matthew 4:1)

Why was Jesus led by the spirit to be tested in the wilderness? What is so important about the wilderness? The children of Israel were tested in the wilderness. John the Baptist was a voice crying out in this same place. Why? The wilderness is a place not meant to be inhabited by man. Wild beast and predators dwell here.

This is a place symbolic of the life cravings of the flesh, or our carnality. The word carnal, derives from the word carnivorous which means flesh eater.

"So, I say, walk by the Spirit, and you will not gratify the desires of the flesh"

(Galatians 5:16)

God sent John to warn those who live according to things that feed the flesh to come out from what eats at your soul and devours your spiritual life. God sent Christ to show us how to defeat the cravings of the flesh as it is written. (Matthew 4:1-11) God came down from heaven and lived with the children of Israel to guide them from bondage to freedom, from unlawful living to a blessed covenant with Him.

In the jungle of broken humanity, the holy law, and the nature of sin battle for the souls of men. Yet, through it all. God shows us that He will never leave us nor forsake us. Christ was the watering refreshing in the cloud by day, and the purifying fire by night in the wilderness. (Exodus 13: 21-22)

The wilderness saga

Once upon a time there was a small shepherd boy who found himself in the wilderness.

This young child was given a huge responsibility. Within his care was entrusted a precious flock of sheep that this young man took immense pride in caring for and protecting. One day, this earthen treasure was threatened by both a bear and a lion. An amazing thing happened on this day. The child was somehow fearless!

Even though he had never met such a problem before, he was unafraid. Like many of us the lad found himself in a predicament that he could have never imagined. In the wilderness, in the face of death the boy discovered a power that was suddenly available in a crisis, a power that he never knew existed. The lion and bear attacked! With his bare hands the small shepherd boy killed the ferocious predators.

In absolute wonder in the aftermath of such triumph, this young boy stood alone in the shadow of death, surrounded by the noises and dangerous behaviors in the valley of the beast. This environment is not meant to be inhabited by man. The wilderness is an emotionally draining place, a spiritually dehydrated place, a place of isolation, a place where life is not meant to flourish. This is an empty environment; this place is absent the wells of living water to draw from.

In this dark place life is constantly in jeopardy. As the roars of wild beast and animalistic mating calls penetrate the ears of the young shepherd boy, he realizes that everything that has breath in the wilderness are predators.

Each citizen in this place are stalking another's life. From the man with the bow and arrow, to the man with the riffle or the spear. The animals big or small are all looking to kill to eat and survive.

The small boy wondered what had he gotten himself into? The animals lurked silently and loudly. Some lay in wait within tall grass, some are high in the trees, behind rocks, deep in a hole, covered by shallow or deep water, and some were laying openly in the dirt. Animals, deadly in attack moved with the scent of the wind, sniffing out weakness, while others were hovering around the wounded and hurt.

Vultures of every race were alert; every creature carried a weapon that could end your life in an instant.

The wilderness is a killing field, a testing place, the ultimate battle within. This question faces humanity daily. Can you overcome the desire to conform to the beast like nature of behavior? Can man avoid the desire to take, to stalk, and to attack others for what they want in life without having to work for it? Or will man listen to the still small voice within that is sent not to condemn or judge but to draw you away from darkness?

"As it is written within the book of Elias, the prophet saying, the voice of one crying out in the wilderness, prepare ye' the way of the Lord, make its path straight."

The snakes slither looking to strike! The fangs of dangerous situations reveal itself. The poison is released from drugs, from bottles of alcohol, from sweet lips of prostitutes asking you out for a date. The venom drips in seduction from the poll of strippers, unsuspecting poison is slowly killing so many who venture into the wilderness trying to fulfill their carnal needs.

"For the lips of the adulterous woman drip honey, and her speech is smoother than oil.'
(Proverbs 5:3)

The plethora of beautiful snakes move more crafty, subtle, and alluring than any other creature. This magnetic charm and sex appeal seem harmless, her appeal, sexiness, and voluptuous figure ensnares and traps through the pull of lust and fornication.

The serpents bite is deadly!

In the wilderness there's handsome well-dressed serpents with pistols waiting to rob and kill. Warning, warning, perilous times are among us. Police are shooting unarmed men. Racist couples carry protest signs and demand to make America great again! Anti-blacks demand to return to a time when blacks could not vote, own property, own firearms to protect their family, sleep with white women, or have riches.

Serpents quote scriptures to mislead those caught up in the jungles of life with false doctrine.

Name it and claim it preachers are buying jets and laughing their way to the bank off the sweat of man's brow. The wilderness is a ruthless and ungodly place of corrupt politicians and shyster lawyers.

Yet, the small boy understands the magnitude of his dilemma. He is overwhelmed by his humanness and vulnerability. He understands that he cannot survive in this place alone. The shepherd boy realized that his victories over the predators of the wilderness were not due to his own prowess and abilities.

The lad's life had been touched. He gazed up into the sky and beheld the splendor of the stars, and the powerful heat of the sun. Everywhere his eyes looked he saw the mighty mass of sculptured mountains hewn by the work of God. Raging rivers flowed with such elegance yet carried extreme power that could snatch you with its currents and end your life in a second. The beauty of the peacock mingled with the sleek allure of the puma.

The noise of crashing rhinos frightened men to the core. These sounds of the wilderness screamed out at the young shepherd.

"You don't belong here!" Yet, the galaxies above seemed to whisper. There is a divine purpose That I have for you.

"That I may confirm the oath that I have sworn to your fathers, to give them a land flowing with milk and honey, as at this day."

(Jeremiah 11:5)

"Marcus Garvey led black American's out of the wilderness of self-hatred and despair. In an age of global independence, Garvey was ahead of his time. He saw the future world being divided into racial and economic blocks." Tony Sewell.

There is a promise and a seal of protection for all of humanity, but we must leave Sodom and Gomorrah. We must exodus the wilderness. Today is the day of salvation if we hearken to His voice. Within the concrete jungles of Detroit, Chicago, Baltimore, Cleveland Ohio, Newark, California, and Houston, life can end in an instant.

Everyone is on the take. The herbivore wants something. The carnivore wants something. The hunter wants something. The sexual predator wants something. Be not ignorant of the wiles of the devil. Mating calls come from all forms of life. Phone calls of perversion ring late at night. Calls of adultery early in the morning awakens some. The call of pornography is heard during one's lunch break. The wilderness is always active with those on the prowl. Yet, there is also a lot of beauty here. However, we must not live by sight but by faith, and spiritual discernment.

What looks good can kill you! What taste good can be poisonous. What feels good can be masked with diseases and the deadly attacks of jealousy, greed, and promiscuity.

Many times, I have found myself in the wilderness, being forced to ask myself. How did I get here? How did I end up in the drunk tank, in a jail cell, in a woman's bed I don't remember being with, empty pockets hours after payday, in a brawl with a stranger, or in the adult film store?

Often, we question ourselves or other's when the answer is found in the actions of a little shepherd boy who discovered the beauties of creation, the power of nature, the dangerous elements of life, and the vast resources that come from a position of trust and surrender. Trapped in fascination and gripped by captivation. Who better to ask than the one who is responsible for creating all of this?

David, the little shepherd boy, would later slay both Goliath, and many armies in his battles for the kingdom of God. Despite his many sins David would later be referred to as a man after God's own heart. This mighty man of both Israel and Judah would one day be crowned King. Yet, today, he was none of these things. He had to become. Who are you today? And who will you become through growth and development? Even in his young age he had the manifold wisdom to ask God this important question that is revealed in (Psalms 8:4) "What is man that you are mindful of him? And the son of man that you should visit him?

CHAPTER SIX

SELF- EVALUATION

"The greatest enemy of knowledge is not ignorance; it is the illusion of knowledge." Stephen Hawking

"If we have no peace, it is because we have forgotten that we belong to each other." Mother Teresa

America. I challenge you to examine ourselves as a nation of people, and as a people of morality and character. As we venture into this new presidential administration in a battered and torn nation, how will we heal from the devastation of broken human relations? God is a God of love, and those who follow Him are a people of love. Even those who claim no religion or spiritual lifestyle need love.

When will we discard the hate? As the holidays approach us, the beautiful season of both Thanksgiving and the celebration of the birth of Christ, is love possible among the citizens of America? With so many church buildings being closed, are the doors of the Christian heart still open to pour out her love unto the lost and wayward soul?

We surely cannot go on hoping for a brighter tomorrow with hearts full of hatred and revenge.

Therefore, if we have turned the corner with this election, as we venture throughout life's new horizon looking to love and to be loved by that special someone for the special someone inside of us, can we reflect the persona of Jesus?

In the exodus of 2020, we are striving for a more sanitary and healthier 2021. As we journey down different paths in search for happiness, or to simply become that moment of bliss when love is shared, accepted, and given in mutual respect, intimacy, surrender and sensual delight; many things will still vex the human spirit. If we truly seek equality, harmony of community, a sense of normalcy in the form of social construct, or fair and equal wages in the job market seeking a stronger and vibrant economy for all families across America, we cannot overlook the lost soul or the spiritually disenfranchised, the at-risk children, the homeless, the drug addict, the alcoholic, the single parent, and the impoverished living in marginalized areas of absolute poverty.

As I look at the news, the death toll of COVID-19 is staggering. The people of this nation are soon to experience the taking away of their free will with the forced vaccine shots in cities like New York, and California. As I evaluate myself in comparison with life on the news, and with the life I know in my community, I can clearly see what is ugly, amid what can be so beautiful.

I can see people looking for love amid chaos, romance during infidelity, and financial provision during a period of gambling and a fallen stock market.

I have a great concern as I look at our nation seeking fortune in the midst of selfishness, and improper child rearing, in the midst of babies having babies, while the educated, mature, and industrialized women are aborting our future. I look out across the globe and I wonder like King David. What am I when it comes to the real scheme of things? What am I in comparison to the galaxies and the sum of creation? What is man that God should be mindful of him? Should the Lord care as we riot and loot? As we burn down stores and shout racial epithets at one another?

Should God care about man as they bomb one another in the Middle East, as religious organizations torch churches, and the pope endorses same sex unions even though the Bible in Leviticus 18:22 is contrary to this Catholic promotion of homosexuality?

What is man that God should be mindful of him, when we are not mindful of our Lord and Savior Jesus Christ?

Turning off the television I am compelled to ask myself how can I be effective? If my relationship with Jesus is personal, then I must take what is happening to His children personally and do something about it.

**"Let this mind that was in Christ Jesus, also be in you. Thinking not of yourselves, but on the things of others."
(Philippians 2:5)**

Why should God care for those who seemingly no longer care for themselves? Open the doors to your home, the ones that are heavily barred with armor guard, living in fear of thy neighbor. Walk out into the streets and you are welcomed by wickedness, the viciousness of life and personal indifference. This aura of ill souls and infected spirits is what we have created. As we look for hope, where do we begin within this land of drug deals, trafficking bodies, stolen cars, home invasions, judges taking bribes, and politician's breaking laws they swore to keep.

The question of King David echoes louder than at any other time span in human history. What is man that you are mindful of him? We are who Christ gave His life for. We are Peter who had rejected Christ, yet Jesus still chose to visit him in his spirit and save his soul.

I can hear the voice of Jesus call out...all you who are weary, heavy laden with sin. Cast all your cares upon me for I care for you. I will give you rest.

Come unto me if you are tired of divorce, of failure, of poverty, of sickness, of loneliness, of anger, or mental disorders. Come to me if you need peace, mercy, forgiveness, grace, love, and prosperity.

If you are tired of broken promises and shattered dreams. Come to the altar. I will cover your sins and throw them in the sea of forgetfulness to recall them no more.

God answers David question by how He treats us every day. Man is the object of His love, the apple of His eye, the creation of His heart's content, the treasures of heaven stored up in earthen vessels, and His inheritance of eternity. Man is God's voice in the earth, he is the Lord's purse, wallet, and provision for the poor.

Man has a responsibility upon his shoulders. Like David, the small shepherd boy who found himself in a situation that was too big for him to overcome, too dangerous for him to survive, too vast for him to understand, and too powerful for him to destroy without the leadership and coverings of God. David realized that even the victories over the lion and the bear had been a result of something much bigger than him.

When David slayed Goliath with a slingshot and a small stone, he felt inside that he was empowered by a spiritual force.

As David evaluated himself and posed the question what is man that you should be mindful of him. He was reflecting on the night that he unlawfully took another man's wife in adultery, had a man murdered at war, in addition to the crimes against humanity that he had committed alongside being a bad father when his son Amnon raped his daughter Tamar. David knew that he was unworthy of being King. Yet, he was blessed.

Like many of us, I am forced to ask the question. Why do you love me after all that I have done? Why have you invested such a heavy price by having your only begotten son die for me? When the Lord gave me this anointed message to release through this narrative. He told me this. "People give birth to people. God gives birth to purpose. You can kill a person, but you cannot kill purpose." God is the potter, and we are the clay. We can become born again and transformed from a defeated foe into a mighty man of valor walking in the victory of Christ.

This generation of men are struggling to find purpose, and losing the battle of overcoming the traps and promises of the wilderness which are the snares of the world, or the system that is contrary to the will of God. 2020 has in some regard been coined a fatherless generation. Is this true?

Jesus said it this way. "Be not like Cain, a son of disobedience, whose father was the devil." A bad tree produces bad fruit, but a good tree produces good fruit. Christ also said this." I am the true vine you are the branches." Notice that He said I am the "True vine". Which means there is another vine that you can connect to and reproduce of its kind. * See (Genesis 1:11) There are two spiritual fathers working in the earth. Let us look at this.

"Ye' are of your father the devil, and the lust of your father ye will do.

He was a murderer from the beginning, and abode not in the truth, because there is no truth in him. When he speaketh a lie, he speaketh of his own; for he is a liar, and the father of it" (John 8:44)

Jesus stated: "I tell you the truth, the son can do nothing by himself; he can only do what he sees his Father doing, because whatever the Father does the son also does." (John 5:19)

So, who is your Father? Men, I challenge you to stand up and become the mighty men of valor that God created us to be. We have a promise that is found in (Joshua 1:4) The Lord says. "Be strong and of good courage, be not afraid neither dismayed for the Lord is with you wherever you go!

Men hear me. You have a Father that loves you. You have access to a Father that sits upon the throne of creation and sees your every need.

He is concerned about you. There is nothing too small or too big for Him to handle. Just trust Him. Genuinely believe and turn to yourself from the spirit within you which is of God. All things are possible with Christ Jesus. As we approach the year of 2021, no longer accept the labels that other people attach to you no matter what you have done in your past. God's mercy is new every day.

Men, Your Father would like to tell you this face to face one day. "Well done my good and faithful servant"

We are more than overcomers we are conquerors through Christ Jesus. We are mighty men of valor!

CHAPTER SEVEN

WOMAN UPON THE THRONE

Jasmine turned to her mother. Many things were troubling her. At the tender age of seventeen, she was considered intelligent and very mature. In fact, some have said that she has what the elder generation call an old soul.

"Momma, I feel like a fish out of water when I'm around other women my age. They listen to Nikki, Cardi B, Meagan the Stallion, or Jay-Z. Yet, I do not agree with their messages even though the beats sound good. They wear clothes that leave nothing to the imagination, and all they care about is boys."

Felona sat down the washcloth after drying the last dish and responded to her daughter. She took a deep breath and pondered two things that she had learned from her favorite author, before responding.

> "I really don't think life is about the I-could-have-been. Life is only about the I -tried -to-do. I don't mind the failure, but I can't imagine that I'd forgive myself if I didn't try."

> "If now isn't a good time for truth I don't see when we'll get to it."
>
> Nikki Giovanni

"Baby listen to your momma. But before I comment on what your concerns are. Let me ask you a question. Why does it matter what other girls do or don't do?"

"Momma. You raised me to think about the welfare of other people, especially women. You instilled within me to think in terms of sisterhood. Therefore, when I look at how my sisters are living it's scary."

Felona interjected. "Why such a drastic word as scary?"

"Well…I believe that women are the key to our future generation. The next great, or the next bum, will come from our wombs. Therefore, it matters what type of men we allow to deposit their life seed within our garden. The Bible tells us not to be unequally yoked with unbelievers.

God articulates to women that the man who He created for us is a king, and a man who is the mirror image of His divine character and purpose. With that said Momma, The music, the provocative dress, the dirty movies they talk about, and the wild parties they attend will influence what type of man they marry or sleep with in general."

"Jasmine. I understand how you feel. But your classmates are young. Do not give up on them. We are all sinners saved by grace. None of us, and that means you too. None of us have arrived, and none of us are perfect. Today's music is not my particular choice. But it bespeaks of the times that we live in. And as for the style of dress, as long as you are modest in your apparel what does it matter at the end of the day?"

"Mom. I want a boyfriend like the other girls. I would like to attend the prom, Sweetest Day, and Valentine dances, and go out on dates on weekends. But there is just so much pressure to make out. I tried getting online just to see what is out there besides the boring dudes in my school. I hurried up and got off social media."

"Jasmine, what sites did you go on? Maybe you just had an unpleasant experience, which doesn't mean that they are all bad."

"I went on Tiktok, Instagram, Periscope, and WhatsApp. It was simply crazy!

The girls my age was half naked, offering to do any and everything beneath the sun for money on their cash app. I'm just not about that life Momma. It's hard being a young Christian."

"Jasmine, the life of an Afro-American woman can be hard. Looking at you I think of something that the late great Winnie Mandela said in her book: "Lives of Courage: Women for a New South Africa."

This is what she said. "The years of imprisonment (equivalent to America's slavery) hardened me…I no longer have the emotion of fear… there is no longer anything I can fear. There is nothing the government has not done to me. There isn't any pain I haven't known."

"That's a lot to grasp and soak in momma."

"Yes, it is. However, loving black men can be painful. I love our brothers, but daughter you are a queen. You cannot settle for less than the best that God has created you to love. The world has beaten the black man down in America. It is hard for them to walk with their heads held high. We are often denied the best jobs, and the accommodating housing for safe living outside the ghetto. Brothers are often seen as criminals, thugs, lazy, unemployed, abusive, and dishonest. No. it is not fair, and of course this does not apply to all black men. But the psychological chains of slavery must be broken.

Our justice system is against us, and the odds of success is against us. So, my advice to you is this. Stay celibate, stay a woman of virtue, and stay prayed up. God will send you the king that will reign within your heart. However. Your man must be worthy of giving yourself to. He must be the head through loving leadership not because he has money, strong sexuality, and a misogynistic ego."

"Thanks momma. I needed to hear that. The fact is, I am just not ready to accept what God has not sent me yet. I will not be with just any man to dodge being lonely. The devil is a lie! I need to get a college education and have myself ready for the right guy on my honeymoon night, in addition to being secure financially, with my own home, transportation, good credit, and deeply rooted in the Lord. Momma simply put. God has to be the center of my life from the bedroom to the bank account."

CHAPTER EIGHT

IS LOVE ENOUGH

"He that loveth not knoweth not God; for God is love"
(1 John 4:8)

"Vera, why are you still putting up with Ronnie's mess? What else does he have to do to make you cry? Why are you settling for so much less than what you deserve, on top of allowing him to cause you so much pain? Girl listen to me. I am out here in the workforce where real men handle their business. I am constantly approached on my lunch break or after work by eligible bachelors on a regular basis. So, don't you dare shape your lips to say that all the good men are either married, deceased, or in the penitentiary. That is a lie from the pits of hell.

There are so many worthy men right here in this city. I am speaking about responsible men who would love a smart, sexy, and educated woman such as yourself who make a good income. Vera, you need to shop around for another man. What do you have to lose? Cause that no good man of yours has done nothing for you nor them children that his sorry behind brought into this world!"

"Patricia, you just do not understand."

"Oh, I understand all right. Look at you baby. You think that people cannot see through your caked-on makeup? Girl, I am not trying to hurt your feelings, but I can see the bruises all over your face. That man of yours is abusing you! Look around your house. Go ahead Vera. Look at the emptiness, after all the beautiful things that you worked so hard to buy is missing.

And for what? So, Ronnie can use drugs that you don't even use? That negro sold your stuff for his addiction, and to top it off..."

Vera interjected in disgust.

"Pat please, enough is enough! If you do not have anything good to say about the man that I love, then you can leave my house. You know how I feel about Ronnie."

With a bewildered gaze, Patricia looked at her friend of eighteen years, the woman who stood up for her on the most important day of her life as her maid of honor, the same woman whom she got kicked out of school for due to protecting her from bullies on the playground. How easy one forgets. A deep flush spread across Patricia's face as she recalled the plethora of things that they had been through together as best friends. And to think that Vera was ready to throw it all away for a man. Angry words threatened to spill from her anxious lips. However, she did not wish to abandon their lifetime friendship.

Patricia took a deep breath and let a moment of calm sweep over her before she allowed herself to speak. In a whisper, she spoke from the dept of her heart.

"Vera, you know I love you. I would never do anything intentionally to hurt you. What I want for myself is what I want for you as my sister. I want you to have the best that both God and man has to offer.

I understand that you love Ronnie, but doesn't being in a serious relationship mean that you are entitled to be loved and treated in a special and godly way in return?"

"Pat, Ronnie does love me" Vera jumped in. "Is love enough?"

"I don't know. I admit that we have had our share of problems just like any other couple. Yes, he has stolen from me and he has hit on me. I am not about to excuse his actions. I'm just saying that he only behaves that way when he drinks or get high."

Patricia thought about something that her late mother had always told her about the treatment of people.

"It's very difficult for you to speak out against your child, someone that's in your family, you can have an argument with them, but you can't condemn them. You cannot cast them out because God has not done that to us. We cannot do that to anyone else."
Otis Moss the third

Looking at Vera's shaking lips and noticing the tears about to descend from her eyes, her friend of a lifetime embraced her with support.

"Girl, I can see that you are hurting badly, I'm really sorry. I apologize for being so hard on you; I am just trying to help.

I understand that you probably want to be alone right now to sort things out between you and Ronnie. I love you, and I'm here for you if you wish to converse later."

The two women ended their embrace and briefly gazed into each other's eyes which released a silent message that said loud and clear. We will never allow a man or anything else to come between us.

"Well my sister" Patricia said in a weary voice. "I'm out of here. I need to go pick my babies up from school, go grocery shopping, to the laundry mat, and then child, I need to clean my house it is a wreck!

I will call you later, maybe we can catch a movie, dinner, or just slum in a few clubs and shake our big behinds like we use to while listening to some old school Parliament."

"Ok girlfriend, I'll see you." They hugged one last time before Vera escorted her partner outside to her car. They talked a few more minutes before Vera slowly entered her home and closed the door. Seconds later, looking around her house, her friend's words came back to her like a pointing finger. "Look at this empty house, all the stuff you worked your fingers to the bone to get are missing. Look at your face. People can see through all that caked up makeup."

It was like her universe came crashing down upon her all at once. Emptiness, despair, and heartbreaking loneliness smothered her with great pain. Reminiscent of a broken faucet, the tears of hurt and denial came gushing forth. No one was there to ease the pain. No one was there to wipe away the tears, and sadly enough no one was there to care as she dropped her head in shame…hearing her friend's words echo in her mind. "Is love enough?"

CHAPTER NINE

WHAT IS THE VALUE OF TODAY'S CHURCH IN A GLOBAL PANDEMIC?

"From Bloody Sunday to Black Lives matter, the role of the Black church is shifting"

C.T. Vivian

Young children, young men, elderly men, men in urban cities, men in rural areas, men in suburbia, men, rich or poor educated or unlearned are all in the same boat. Men in America, black men, whether they are walking out of their front doors, leaving their jobs, exiting parent's homes, or visiting stores and sporting events, they often face the same fate. Therefore, these men take each step with trepidation. With each step, these men walk in fear of being gunned down by police even though they are innocent of crime...but yet, they have been condemned and sentenced to die because of those in our society, who have judged that our sin is the color of our skin.

America, why is this our reality in the age of Mega-churches? God has not given us a spirit of fear, but of love, power, and a sound mind.

Why then, don't we walk with our heads held high believing that no weapon formed against us shall prosper? Why do we march in droves to stores that sell armory to purchase pistols and bullet proof vest, instead of marching in the light of truth that says having put on the full armor of God I am protected?

Men, young and old live in fear throughout America. Will I be here to love my wife, children, and grandchildren past tonight, or will I fall victim to the plague of hatred, bigotry, and racism? Fear cripples one's movement of God given freedom. Yet, that same fear gives birth to anger, rage, and a need to seek revenge. The spirit of survival arises and forces man to aim and shoot at that which is a practical everyday threat. Not just to his life, but to the lives of those that he loves, and has a moral obligation and a civil responsibility to protect and support.

For centuries ever since our inception upon the shores of America, the black man has been a target of our historical enemy.

Though we are taught to love and to forgive, though we are taught to take the high road and to work twice as hard to succeed, though we are told to shine our true light even amid darkness, yet, even after inaugurating Barak Obama as president black men are still subjected to human indecencies, social injustices, wicked brutality, and inhumane treatment both verbally and spiritually.

Our sacred ancestors sung old negro spirituals. Today we sing powerful words of praise by highly paid and gifted singers. Yet, change has not come! It seems that the pages of history have been resurrected and the portals of time has been reversed and relived vigorously like never before.

Instead of white men wearing sheets, we see business men in suits and behind pulpits executing acts of cruelty, and acts of malicious intent, to wound, to maim, to destroy, and to cripple the will. Racism looks to paralyze the dreams and hopes of a nation of people who simply just want to live. God blew His breath into man and he became a living soul. So, I dare ask. It is too much to ask, or unwarranted to say, "Do not take the breath from us. The breath that God gave us as life."

The world is in a shamble. Why are we living this way? Has the church lost its value? Over seventy million people in America voted for Donald Trump.

Thousands of them were white pastors with churches that are responsible for the education of the spirit man, and the impartation of love into the human soul and heart.

Why do men of God support such a man? We have seen the tweets, the sexist remarks and behavior. We have seen the racist character and slurs directed at African American people. We have seen the lies and tax evasion; we have seen the division that is purposely caused by the former president.

Even in defeat Trump is firing people who opposed him. Even in defeat he is causing divide. Yet, white evangelicals support him. And so, has the church lost its power to love thy neighbor when we see those in pulpits support what God hates. He detests pride, a liar, arrogance, and self-exaltation.

"The fear of the Lord is hatred of evil. Pride and arrogance and the way of evil and perverted speech I hate"
(Proverbs 8:13)

Jesus prayed that we become one. (John 17:21) how can we when the church is separated like never before in a time when COVID 19 is ravishing the country? In a time when the economy is starving businesses, and bankrupting saving accounts and depleting insurance claims for hospitalization.

In a time where families are fallen apart, and unable to visit due to travel bans, quarantine, and social distancing. Has the church lost its value? With its doors closed due to this pandemic, while many leave their homes afraid, seeking peace, mercy, love, understanding, comfort, help, forgiveness, and salvation. Yet, broken people across this nation, downtrodden, weary, looking for rest and the promise of a new birth arrive at a place where the promises were once preached, But the doors are closed. Where can man go? Especially the black man.

CHAPTER TEN

HOW TO PUT ON THE ARMOR OF GOD

(Ephesians 6: 11-17)

As we gaze out into this troubled world with a jaundiced eye, let us be mindful that God has given us the keys to success through the revelatory knowledge found in Ephesians 6:11-17.

> ➤ The first key is having your loins girt with truth. Before I get into the text allow me to give you the definition of the word girt. (Girt, or gird) means to gird oneself for the trial ahead, to provide, equip, or invest, as with power or strength. To encircle or bind with a belt or band. The loins are your reproductive organ.

In this scripture from Ephesians 6:11-17, the word of God instructs us to Gird your loins with truth. In order to fully understand the text, we need to discover what is the Biblical term for truth. John 17:17 gives us the answer. It reads. "What is truth? Thy word is true!"

Therefore, God instructs us in how to use our sexual organs in His word. The beauty of love in the making is not Satan's idea. Lovemaking is a gift from the Lord. Sex is not a perverted union; it is a blessed and anointed copulation of two souls with espoused hearts.

We are blessed to enjoy the pleasures and excitement found within the sacred union of one another according to God's holy covering.

"Marriage is honorable unto all, the marriage bed is undefiled, but whoremongers and fornicators God will judge." (Hebrew 13:4)

God blesses right relationships. When we think about many of the problems that affect our society, we will notice that they are in the lust department. Divorces due to infidelity, sexually transmitted diseases, pornography, homosexuality, and pedophilia are the fruit from the disobedience in how God instructed us to use our sexual organs. If we as a culture would obey this key to success, think of the beauty that we would experience with loving marriages and strong healthy families.

Please take note of this: Marriage is God's expression of humanity that reflects His holiness from heaven.

> ➤ The second key: Having on the breastplate of righteousness. The breastplate is body armor worn by a soldier who is engaged in warfare. This particular part of armor is designed to protect the heart region. In spiritual revelation, the breastplate symbolizes protecting the spirit by guarding what you allow into your life, by rejecting or fighting off things that attempt to enter your soul that are detrimental and harmful. Such as, abusive people, dream killers, negative music, x rated movies, or things that trigger old habits or draw out your worse attributes. In our warfare we must also fight off drugs and false friendships. Both are leeches that take, drain, and use. These false dependencies are illusions of help, when in reality they never enhance or give.

It's prudent that we surround ourselves with people who have our answers; and stay away from those who are a problem to our goals, family, marriage, job, income, spirituality, and hinders our growth and development as a person.

The breastplate allows you to guard your heart and to remain in right standing with God. It is especially important that we protect our heart.

> ➤ The third key: Having your feet shod with the preparation of the gospel of peace. This key is symbolic of the direction of life. The steps of a righteous man are ordered by the Lord. The good news of the gospel is having that inner peace between you and God that was made available through the blood shed of Jesus Christ that made an atonement for the sinful laws that mankind has transgressed. God uses the terminology having your feet shod, to articulate growth, walking, traveling, and taking progressive steps in a certain direction. The Gospel (the good news about Jesus) is the key to life, if we are to move in the right direction of racial unity, marital harmony, economic solidarity, and the rebuilding of a divided nation. Only the gospel can turn foes into friends by setting both a loving standard of lawful community and human decency toward all of God's children. When we follow the direction of the Lord, His loving leadership steers us away from evil, while freeing us from the practices of self-destruction. Wrong living weakens a nation's character and harms the people we love. To walk in the spirit is to take mindful steps and to willfully move forward. This is a crucial challenge for this generation. To heal, we must move forward, with the courage and fortitude of uniting in the gospel of national fellowship and humane communion.

> ➤ The fourth key: The shield of faith.

The purpose of this sacred concept is believing in a higher standard of life that protects the emotions and physical safety of others, which is very important while dealing with people, especially those who have different backgrounds, different beliefs, and opposite doctrine. Faith, or a lack of faith has divided many people. * Note: Authentic faith is not blind faith. By God's definition a person has faith because of substance and evidence that has been demonstrated by who or what the person has faith in (Hebrew 11:1) (i.e.) how could my faith in a statue be real faith? The statue cannot hear, speak, touch, taste, feel, nor create. Therefore, believing in a statue or idol has no valid power to change me nor my situation.

Right thinking is centric for esteemed behavior. Trusting in what God has spoken, decreed, declared, pronounced, promised, or ordained and proven throughout history is having faith and being confident in who God is and in who He made us to be. This type of faith is assured that all things will work together for our good, if we have placed our present, and future care within the directive care and wisdom of the Lord.

Our gifts, talents, skills, and capability to understand and perform is derivative from God. When we apply faith in one another to achieve a certain task, or to love faithfully, in essence, we are not trusting the person, but the spirit that dwells within the woman or man.

America is in shambles due to the disjointed spirituality that is displayed from person to person. What we see when we look at each other is the harvest of our treatment towards one another, which is contrary to the teachings of Christ.

Let us examine two powerful scriptures that bear witness to this truth.

"The earth will become desolate because of its inhabitants, as the result of their deeds." (Micah 7:13)

"This is my commandment that you love one another, even as I have loved you." (John 15: 12)

➤ The Fifth key: The helmet of salvation. This powerful phrase opens our eyes to the importance of renewing how we think.

Renewing the mind from the state of being carnal minded is possibly the most important key to our personal change, and our change as a nation, or community. The first message that Jesus preached was "repent" for the kingdom of heaven is at hand. The word repent means to re-think, or reconsider. In order for our behaviorism toward one another to change, serious and significant alterations need to take place through how we think about the value of one another. To rebuild what has been torn down after the progressive tenure of Barak Obama, we must acknowledge the need to work together across racial, political, and church denominations.

If you wonder how this can be accomplished, think on the things that God condones, blesses, empowers to prosper, and apply it to your life.

"Finally, brothers and sisters, whatever is true, whatever is noble, whatever is right, whatever is pure, whatever is lovely, whatever is admirable-if anything is excellent or praiseworthy-think about such things."
(Philippians 4:8)

Guard your thought life, invest in how you think, by studying, through education, and by stimulating your mind with mental food, reading, and conversing with positive and smart people.

It would be wise in my opinion to befriend and associate with good people who share in your ideologies. Iron sharpens iron. For my own personal growth, I understand that God's word is quintessential to having life and life more abundantly. As a man, the leader of my home, I need to be well informed in how to lead. Jesus led by following the Father's plan of reconciliation. When we study how Jesus thought we will see that He wore the helmet of salvation. This important key is symbolic through imagery which depicts an object that prevents head injuries.

Having on the helmet of salvation protects you from adopting bad thinking. Wrong thinking is the fuel that empowers criminal and detrimental behavior.

> ➤ The Sixth key: The sword of the Spirit. This part of warfare is correspondent with both faith and with what direction in life you will take. Also, this key is imperative if you are going to renew your mind daily. The sword of the spirit is symbolic for the active living word of God. To effectively use this method of spiritual warfare is to take initiative, and attack with the word. I have learned to arm myself with the word of God, instead of waiting for things to happen, and then try to pray my way out, pray through, or pray the Lord into the situation, I cover myself first, I rebuke disease, and bind sickness even while I am healthy. This initiative-taking mindset defuses the power of the enemies'

attack. I pray for traveling mercies, and financial prosperity. I pray for guidance and open doors in business ventures. When dealing with people I ask for divine favor. I cover my family each night in the holy blanket of prayer. I have learned too that the word will instruct us in marriage, stewardship, and in how to effectively deal with the enemy. A peaceful mind is a weapon against anger. Love disarms hate. A sound mind is a weapon against actions of haste and preconceived notions.

The word is your key to open up life.

Let us examine a few scriptures that changed my life, and how I view the word of God which is the sword of the Spirit.

"It is the Spirit that quickened (gives life); the flesh (opposition to the spirit of God) profited nothing: the words that I speak unto you, they are spirit and life." (John 6:63)

"The entrance of the word giveth light and understanding even to the simple." (Psalm 119:130)

"Forever O Lord, thy word is settled in heaven, and established in the earth." (Psalm 119:89,90)

Jesus lets us know in John 6:63 that His anointed word gives life. His words are spiritual, and never worldly.

His words are always the Fathers will. Therefore, what He speaks is our spiritual purpose and fulfilled promises.

Psalms 119:89,90 informs us that every conclusion of a situation has been figured out by what God has already said from heaven.

Why did Jesus make this statement in Matthew 6:8. He spoke these words "Thy will shall be done on earth, as is it in heaven" This is the divine will of the Father. Therefore, when I need to know something, or if I am faced with something and I am not sure of what to do…

I search the word. I have matured to understand that there is no better source of wisdom, knowledge, or education than a word from the Lord. It is such a blessing and a matchless source of knowledge to know that whenever I bring the word of God into any situation, it will change!

The word gives life to dead situations and spiritually dead people. You can pray for lost loved ones, and they can be saved due to the Lord responding to your prayer. Yes, we have a free will, yet God can draw that person with an overwhelming love.

In my personal life, I can bear witness to the power of the word. As a delivered addict, I can tell those in recovery that the power of the word will transform addiction to sobriety. I can tell you that truth within the word of God is not packed with elements of the world, but with treasures and healing agents from the throne in the kingdom.

Things of the world will crumble, decay, diminish, and deceive. This is a priceless word for those who may be struggling in their relationships. The word of God will resurrect a dying marriage between man and God and between woman and man.

The word of God gives us access into the presence of God and grants us the opportunity to both fellowship together and to cross over into enemy territories and save those trapped in bondage to Satan.

Through the sacred word of God, we must confront, and deal with the mortality rate in America that is erasing our children in record numbers. We must discontinue enriching funeral homes, prisons, and life insurance companies with the lives of our youth who are dying too early in the streets of this country. We must pick up the word (our sword) and fight!

This is our challenge. If tomorrow will become different, we must transform through the word and not conform to a hopeless plight or a dismal future that causes more tears in the graveyard. If we apply Ephesians 6: 11-17 our lives and our nation will change.

CHAPTER ELEVEN

VISION

Divorce is too common. The high rate of abandoned children or single parenthood is too prevalent to dismiss or ignore. The conditions of unemployment and poverty are too vast among young men. Mass incarceration is too embedded in our culture. Lack of leadership is too cavalier in our manly households. Domestic violence and early deaths are fixtures in our reality, especially in our urban experience.

So, the question is, why are these conditions part of the norm and not a rarity? I believe that in many cases, we have failed in our pursuits to overcome and conquer detrimental elements in our life due to not knowing what to do in response to certain things, and by not knowing what or how to give in certain moments of grief, adversity, death, or broken heartedness. Often, I believe that we fail in not knowing when to be silent, or when to speak with God given authority.

Often, in parental guidance and as husbands we do not discern the difference between when money or our presence is needed. What we need is vision. However, please understand that bad eyesight does not mean that you are a bad person. A lot of us react according to how we were raised, peer pressure, our environment, bad influences, and according to our culture and systemic beliefs.

Jesus healed the blind. Therefore, we need education in the ways of seeing and acknowledging our creative purpose. In a crucial time in his life King David was blind to what direction he needed to move in to gain success over the enemy, so he asked God to teach his hands to war. The king's petition was a request for knowledge to fight in a way that will ensure victory. Blindness hinders correct direction in life.

Therefore, I hope that this brief but meaningful dialogue of the spirit within this chapter will encompass what God has to say about us, why His words are so important to our success, and why we cannot achieve our potential greatness without His leadership and loving protection.

Vision is the key. Ephesians 1:18 Apostle Paul understood this, he prayed, "I pray that the eyes of your understanding be enlightened".

Vision for those who want to see as God sees

The definition of vision has six important components

- Divine revelation
- The faculty or state in having the ability to see
- Having the tools that make sight possible
- The revelation of what you are seeing is being spiritually discerned
- The ability to think about or plan the future with imagination and wisdom
- A picture that is not actually present, but is seen in your mind

(Proverbs 29:18) Where there is no vision, the people perish, but he that kept the law, happy is he.

The first vital point in the above text is that spiritual blindness comes from not keeping the law of God, the spiritual principles of how the kingdom of heaven works. When Adam disobeyed the spoken word of the Lord, he lost everything that was in God's presence that pertained to God's kingdom of provision, protection, and permission. Once Adam accepted a plan other than the Lord's he became mentally blind.

He no longer thought like God, spoke God's faith language, or acted like God. Adam perished when he disagreed with the Lord's instructions due to imagining Satan's vision was a better life than what God had to offer.

When we think of vision the first thing that usually come to mind is eyesight. Yet, vision entails so much more than physically seeing.

The definition for vision according to the word of God is "divine revelation." Therefore, being able to see things clearly in your life, will be determined by the level of divine revelation that you gain. Men are failing in vital areas due to a lack of God's wisdom. This type of ignorance is not intellectual. Certain failures are a result of not being properly enlightened by the word of God about a particular subject or thing.

(Psalms 119: 130, says the entrance of the word gives light and understanding to the simple. The terminology for light is illumination, enlightenment, awareness, and God knowledge. When what God has spoken enters the conversation or situation, things change.

(John 1:4) states that Jesus is the life of man and His life is the light of humanity. The example Christ set through how He gave, lived, and loves, is the light that gives us the divine revelation on how we are to love, lead, educate, instruct, submit, and fellowship with one another. In the book of Genesis 1:1 God said let there be Light. This statement was in response to an earthly problem. The world was without void, form, life, and it was covered in complete darkness. This earthly condition was contrary to the vision that God had for His creation. Therefore, He spoke a spirit filled word which carried a heavenly solution, changing the earthly problem that was opposing His divine will. The word of God is both spirit and life. (John 6:63)

Vision is being able to see the solution to a problem and knowing what to do through spiritual insight. (i.e.) how did Adam name the animals that God created? He had God knowledge. He was created in The Lord's image and likeness.

Philippians 2:5 gives sage advice as it reads," let the mind that was in Christ Jesus also be in you". The first message that Jesus preached was repent, which means to re-think! Therefore, our mentality must change when it comes to how we confront problems.

Vision is also foresight being able to see the outcome before the act. (i.e.) God says in Malachi 3:8-11 if we tithe or bring ten percent of our earnings into His storehouse that He will open up the window of heaven and pour out a blessing more than we can receive. This is a promise for the sower of the financial seed. Therefore, when you receive the harvest that God promised it should not come as a surprise or as a shock.

We should look at giving with a spirit of expectancy because God's word is a promise, and He is not a man that He should lie. True vision is expecting the things that God promised.

Praise the Lord, I can plan things in my life to take place because I believe that God is in control and that He is directing my steps. The word says that the word is both a lamp (illumination in my present time and circumstance) and a light upon my path (future direction) as I travel in my journey throughout life.

The Bible says that God is love. Therefore, everything that He does is because of love. Discipline is out of love. Prosperity is out of love. What the Lord speaks is out of love. "He that loveth not, knoweth not God; for God is love." (1 John 4:8) Jesus said in John 13: 35 "you will know my disciples if they love one another". The word Disciple means those who have learned from Christ, who have been taught personally by His Spirit, and those who follow the Father in their actions.

It is vitally important that we understand that love is not an emotion. It is an action response. It will greatly enrich our lives if we grasp that love should always have a destination. Each day that we wake up we are being led by love. When Jesus said, "follow me," He began to do, then teach. (Acts 1:1) Christ showed us the Father by how He treated us. He said, "when you see me you see the Father." First the word comes and then a vision of what the words is.

Genesis 15:1 reads: "After these things the word of the Lord came to Abram in a vision, saying fear not, Abram, I am your shield, your abundant compensation, and your reward shall be great."

We see from the following text that vision speaks to you about where God is taking you. Vision ministers to your soul.

What God reveals should reassure us not to look at things with regular eyesight but with the eyes of faith and trust in His word. Let us examine the following text. Revelation 21:4 The new Jerusalem is a vision given to John. This vision is first: a revelation about who Jesus is.

Secondly, this divine vision gives us sight into God's kingdom and the purpose of it. A revelation unfolds our future. The eternal promises of the Lord are designed to keep us encouraged and full of hope. The word of God firmly proves that we have the final victory.

Vision is the unveiling of divine mysteries. The book of Amos 3:7 states that God does nothing without first revealing it to His prophets (or those He sends with a message) A vision is being in a spiritual place mentally.

Ephesians 4:23 Articulates this point as it reads: To be made new in the spirit of your mind. Men of God, how you mentally see things will determine your physical actions.

Love leads you to a place where there is no death. Love does not cause you to do things that will cause separation from the Lord.

Within the manifestation of love, or the fruit of love, there should be no tears of heartache or unhappiness. God is love. Therefore, there should be no darkness or evil in your marriage or relationship.

Our lives should not be lived in ways contrary to Gods word and commandments. Jesus said, "if you love me you will keep my commandments." (John 14:15)

Where love exists, there is no sickness or disease. Meaning: Such ailments or pathologies are things that deteriorate the relationship, things that eat at you from the inside and cause your marriage to implode. Implosion is when things die from the workings of what is happening in the house. Such as, lack of intimacy, abuse, lack of communication, lack of financial support, or infidelity. These things cause spiritual dis-ease and disrupts peace and unity. A house that is divided cannot stand.

Spouses must have the same vision about who God is to become one in both purpose and destination through the plan of salvation. If couples have separate visions that's Di-vision or two visions. Therefore, when this happens, they grow apart instead of together. When Christ entertained the thought that there might be another way to save humanity without going to the cross, He was having a different vision than the Father. Nevertheless, He got back into their oneness and said. "not my will, but thy will be done."

For the word was already settled in heaven. (Psalms 119:89.90 "for without the shedding of innocent blood there is no remission of sins." Christ came to fulfill the law not abolish it.

To succeed as humankind, we must have vision. Let us not lean to our own understanding but acknowledge God in all our ways and He will direct our path. (Proverbs 3: 5-6)

CHAPTER TWELVE

FIVE BUILDING BLOCKS

1. Why does it matter: I believe that there are two vitally important scriptures that are crucial in gaining both promotion and endorsement from the Lord? In Philippians 2:5 the word of God articulates equality of mindset. It reads, "let the mind that was in Christ Jesus also be in you."

The second text is found in Psalms 119:89,90. This holy writ expresses being joined to the wisdom and results of God.

The text reads: "thy word has been forever settled in heaven O Lord, and forever proven in the earth."

If you were to enjoin these two sacred texts you will conclude that the mindset of Jesus is thinking on the things that are written by God as a way of life that we are to live according to the plan and will of the Father. For Christ to be successful in His pursuit of saving humankind from destruction and eternal damnation He had to follow the plan of salvation set forth by the Father. Therefore ultimately, if we are to succeed in anything lasting and meaningful, we should know what God's will is concerning our business or personal endeavors. Everything that God does is with both great significance and divine purpose. Therefore, in your quest for achievement ask yourself whose life will my work or service impact? Who else besides me will prosper financially? Always remember that divine blessings involve the helping of others. Selfishness has no place in the plan of God. The Scriptures tell us that Abraham, the father of faith is blessed to be a blessing. 1 Corinthians 13:2 gives us true vision on what should be the center and reason for our endeavors. God is no respect of persons He has his whole creation in mind when He speaks and act.

In the above text, Apostle Paul states that if I have the gift of prophecy and can fathom all mysteries and all knowledge, and if I have a faith that can move mountains, but do not have love, I am nothing.

This is a key point to understand. We can accumulate wealth and possessions, but if my life does not produce love for myself, family, and for humanity, Paul said, "I am nothing."

Why would Apostle Paul say such a profound statement concerning himself? 1 John 4:7-21 tells us that God is love. the Apostle is letting us know that if he achieves anything outside of God's word, ways, or character then he has no substance as a person. (i.e.) If I was a drug dealer and broke down 36 ounces from a kilo of cocaine into 50,000 $20 rocks and sold them what type of person would I be? Think about this for a minute. This would be my mentality. Remember the word of God says as a man thinketh so is he!

If I am willing to damage 50 thousand lives just to put money in my pocket. What does that say about my character?

Especially when I know ahead of time the damage that drugs have on its users. We can visibly see this destruction in the world around us daily. People overdose and die from drugs. They lose jobs, lose custody of their children, develop serious health problems, commit crimes to support their addiction, sell their bodies to get high, and suffer years of social problems and broken relationships with family and friends.

The following statement makes it clear. "Where there is a lack of vision my people perish." Lack of seeing human value breeds hatred and selfishness.

Paul understands that the significance of what we do and the impact it has on people matters. If we do not pursue things out of love, or without God's intended will for His children it is not worth doing.

2. Warfare mentality: Strategy is necessary! You must have a plan to get to where you want to go in business, relationships, investments, and in the need department.

Proverbs 3:5-6 reads: "Trust in the Lord with all thine heart; and lean not unto your own understanding. In all thy ways acknowledge Him, and he shall direct thy paths". To succeed it is imperative that we have God knowledge. What do I mean by God Knowledge? The Lord created animals, but Adam named them. (Genesis 2:19) Adam looked at the behavior of the animals and discerned their nature and properly named them accordingly. The serpent who is the Devil or Satan is said to be more cunning than any creature. This is his nature and behaviorism. Jesus said my children know my voice. Therefore, once again consider why I mentioned the drug dealer earlier. Is being a bar owner a righteous endeavor? Or a strip club?

Evaluate the nature of your dreams. Look at the characteristics of your vision. What does it say about whatever it is that you are wishing to do? Reiterating Proverbs 3:5-6 Following the Lord will result in the destination of God's purpose for you.

3. Design is the pattern of your vision: Structure your goals according to your gifts, financial ability, insight revelations, and final outlook projections. Your goals are merely seen as a pattern and a foreshadowing of what has its true existence and reality in the heavenly sanctuary. For when Moses was about to erect the tabernacle, he was warned by God, saying see to it that you make it all exactly according to the copy the model which was shown to you on the mountain. (Hebrew 8:5)

God will show you what your purpose is, how to achieve your goals, and place the right people in your life to solidify your project. You will never succeed outside of your gift.

Your gift will make room for you and bring you before kings and great men. Not because they are great, but because you have been restored to your rightful purpose by God and is on the right track. * See Revelations 1:6-8

4. Measure your sight: Meaning, can you see the acorn tree while it is still in seed form? The word of God says that you will know my children by their fruit. Measure your vision by its God potential, spiritual productivity, and by the abilities to bless others in longevity. God's blessings are not temporal. Love is not just for a season. Provision is not momentarily. If you were to study McDonalds, Goodyear's tire Company, Walmart, or Levi jeans, these businesses have been around for decades because they have the service of everybody intended. They do not just cater to a particular group of people. Remember God is no respect of persons.

True ministry like businesses will affect and support humanity. If God is for you the vision will flourish, increase, expand, and prosper. "The blessings of the Lord it makes truly rich, and he adds no sorrow with it neither does toiling increase it." (Proverbs 10:22)

God shows us according to the above text that He will increase your vision by His will and purpose for you. Your own efforts cannot and will not cause increase. Also * see Genesis 1:28

5. Be constant and devoted: Galatians 5:22-23 tells us that the fruit of the spirit is love, joy, peace, longsuffering, gentleness, goodness, faith, meekness, temperance, against such there is no law. These nine qualities should go with whatever you do in life. Why do I stress this? This fruit or the result of being connected to Christ in spirit will display your character, and how you deal with people. Money and gain are not the most essential elements to success. How you treat people is the most important value and tool that you own.

CHAPTER THIRTEEN

VISION BOARD

1. (Habakkuk 2:2) "and the Lord answered me and said write the vision down and make it plain, that he may run after it that reads it." Your vision should attract people.

   Your purpose should make people want to be a part of what you are doing for humanity. What you do for the Lord will last and bless others.

   You are blessed to be a blessing. Do not procrastinate. Have faith in what God has shown you and act on it with absolute trust in both the journey and the finished process.

   Do not allow obstacles along the way to cause you to doubt your dreams or vision and give up. Remember, all things work together for your good for those who love God and are called according to His will.

2. Know your limitations and reach of power: (Philippians 4:13) "I can do all things through Christ which strengthens me." This is a vital point in any pursuit in life. Apart from Jesus we can do nothing that has value to and for the kingdom. Business oriented people. Look at your vision board both short term and long term. Understand what you can afford, who your staff is, what direction

you need to go in, what your resources are, and who your audience is. Your power is within those God align you to.

The sphere of your influence is where your prosperity lies. (i.e.) a brain surgeon has no value with people who need a plumber.

3. Be unceasing in your approach: Do not be motivated sometimes, or creative now and then, or willing to work hard only for certain clients or times of the year. (Hebrews 13:8) "I am the same yesterday, today, and forever more." God does not take a day off with raising the sun or allowing the wind to blow, or supplying water, gas, and the essentials to sustain life for His creation. Our mindset should be to deliver the best that our vision provides in the areas of application, quality giving, and customer service.

4. (Acts 1:8) "But you shall receive power, after that the Holy spirit is come upon you; and ye shall be witnesses unto me both in Jerusalem and in all Judea, and in Samaria, and unto the uttermost part of the earth." This Christ like vision is understanding that the fulfilling of who God is within your life will empower you to succeed in such a way that you will be a witness for the work of the Lord globally. Notice that this cannot happen until you receive the Holy spirit.

    We are created in the image and likeness of God. Therefore, you cannot have true vision disconnected from the God who created heaven and earth. God will give you resources in the earth from His unlimited heavenly source.

5. Get a thinking partner: Have at least two people that you can trust who you can enjoy in brainstorming sessions, or meetings. Its key that you surround yourself with likeminded people, and with smart people who can stretch you, challenge you, and question you on key points in your endeavors to bring forth a clarity of direction, purpose, and needed outcome. James 5: 16 reads: "Confess your faults one to another, and pray one for another, that you may be healed. The effective fervent prayer of the righteous avails much". Your thinking partner is not your praying partner.

You should have a spiritual link to join with on a regular basis. When Jesus raised a young lady from the dead, the first thing that He conducted was to put out of the room every person who did not have faith in Him and in what He was there to do. We live in the flesh realm, but we think from a spiritual perspective. So, it would be wise to have both a thinking partner and a prayer partner.

6. Be focused. Bad eyesight causes accidents, places you in danger, and causes you to miss the mark repeatedly.

Your vision must not be impaired by things that you can control. Let us examine the following text.

He answered and said I was only sent to the lost sheep of the house of Israel. (Matthew 15:24)

Jesus' focus was on restoring lost children back to the loving relationship of the Father. However, His focus also had depth and scope for others.

Jesus blessed all non-Jews because He was moved by compassion and because He wishes that none should perish. Therefore, your vision should be diverse. It should have different streams of impact. If you have a grocery store you want your food to feed more than just one race of people. You want to appeal to anyone who is hungry and to anyone who enjoys tasty food. As men, our vision should be healthy for our family, and beneficial for the growth and development of society. While man was at his worse God saw into the future where man could live with Him in eternal holiness and enjoy His undying love. Therefore, He sent Christ to redeem us. As men who are the seed of the Lord, we must be able to see as God sees and live by faith trusting in the finished work of Christ, and believe that if we stay the course we will arrive at the place where God leads us to be. In Jeremiah 29:11 God says I know the thoughts I have for you are good and not evil. I have an expected end for you"

When the Lord states that my thoughts of you are good. He is taking us back to the Garden of Eden. Everything that He said was good is meant for us to enjoy today.

7.What are those things? God's presence on a daily basis. A spouse, a loving companion to share and enjoy life with. Healthy foods, a home supported by God. Meaning: you are living according to His will for you. Squalor is not your home. Prosperity is God's will for you. Adam was given a land of gold. Agriculture fed his family in the present. Gold was a future currency. God has both your right now and your future covered. His desired end is eternity with Him, where there is no death, sorrow, tears, sickness, nor a separation from Him.

Family, love, and goodwill fellowship with thy neighbor is the fulfillment of all visions from the Lord.

CHAPTER FOURTEEN

FROM BLINDNESS
TO GOD SIGHT

Through the assignment of the Holy Spirit, I would like to give you four examples of how vision changes the outcome of situations in a drastic way.

This first depiction is the picture of the church. Think about this for a minute. The church, the holy ones chosen by God are blind to who they are, and to what they are capable of being, until the word spoken by the prophet Ezekiel was uttered unto them. Once the church received the word of God their thinking was renewed, they saw themselves differently, and their belief of the Lord changed.

"Then he said unto me, "Son of man, these bones are the whole house of Israel: behold they say, our bones are dried, and our hope is lost: we are cut off from our parts" (Ezekiel 37:11)

The people of God, due to living in sin and being separated from the Lord for so long, felt as though the wrongs that they had committed over a course of time had forever cut them off from the blessings and relationship with the Lord. In the above text, the church said, "we have no hope"! Therefore, the opinion of themselves were one of hopelessness.

Have you ever felt like God would never forgive you for the things that you may have done? Or maybe you heard that the Lord would forgive you, but you thought that He could never use you to teach, preach, or to pray for others. I know that Peter felt that way after rejecting Christ. Why do I say this? The actions of Jesus I believe support my understanding of the narrative.

After resurrecting from the tomb, the first conversation that Christ carried on was with Mary whom He instructed to tell Peter and his disciples that He had risen. Jesus made sure that Peter was included. Peter must have believed that he was forever doomed after rejecting the Lord. However, God shall never leave us nor forsakes us. He always has a plan for His people. Let us look at what happened to a hopeless church. The prophet Ezekiel prophesied a word that was commanded of him, and breath came into them, and they lived, and stood up upon their feet, an exceeding great army (Ezekiel 37:10)

At this moment we can evaluate another story of great report, and watch an incredible change transpire from the following scripture. "And the Lord took me as I followed the flock, and the Lord said unto me, go prophesy unto my people Israel. (Amos 7:15)

God viewed Amos according to the purpose that He had in store for him. Yet, Amos did not see himself as capable or worthy of speaking a word into the lives of the Lord's people.

Then answered Amos, and said to Amaziah, "I was no prophet, neither was I a prophet's son; but I was a herder, and a gatherer of sycamore fruit." (Amos 7: 14)

It is important that we grasp what is transpiring in these sacred scriptures as we continue to see that men view themselves as one way, yet, God sees them according to what He can do through them. Nothing is impossible with God. Praise the Lord. We can do all things through Christ who strengthens us.

This next revelation that I am about to share is an amazing story of mental blindness and a lack of self-esteem. The Lord spoke purpose and change into the way this young man saw himself and the God we serve. And the Angel of the Lord appeared unto him (Gideon) "the Lord is with thee, thou mighty man of valor" (Judges 7:12)

And Gideon said unto him," O my Lord, if the Lord be with us, why then is all this befallen us? And where be all his miracles which our fathers told us about, saying, did not the lord bring us out of Egypt? But now the Lord hath forsaken us and delivered us into the hands of the Midianites." (Judges 7: 13)

"And the Lord said unto Gideon. I will I save you and deliver the Midianites into thy hand; and let all the other people go every man unto his place." Before the victory was given to Gideon by the Lord, God spoke a word into His servant that would cause him to see himself differently. God called him a mighty man of valor. He spoke leadership over this young man's life knowing that one day he would lead an army into victory. How we see God and ourselves will decide our defeats or victories in life.

Lastly, God had spoken to a man by the name of Barak and had instructed him to take ten thousand men and go to mount Tabor. Yet, Barak was afraid to fight even though he had the numbers and had heard from the Lord. How Barak saw himself made him disobey the Lord.

However, Deborah, the prophetess, intervened and said to him, "hath not the Lord commanded saying, go and draw ten thousand men of the children of Naphtali and of the children of Zebulun?"

And Barak said to her, "if thou wilt go with me, then I will go; but if thou wilt not go with me, then I will not go". (Judges 4: 6,8)

"And behold, as Barak pursued Sisera, Jael came out to meet him, and said, "come, and I will show you the man you look for." And when he came into her tent, behold Sisera lay dead, and the nail was in his temple. And the hand of the children of Israel prospered, and prevailed against Jabin the king of Canaan until they had destroyed Jabin king of Canaan." (Judges 4:24)

John 12:45 reads: "And he that see me sees Him that sent me".

Jesus is the way to eternal salvation and the means to everything prosperous. This is the truth that all of humanity must see if we are to excel and become victorious in our lives.

CHAPTER FIFTEEN

CLARITY OF VISION

The eyes of your understanding being enlightened; that you may know what is the hope of your calling, and what the riches of the glory of his inheritance in the saints (Ephesians 1:18)

I will lead the blind by ways they have not known, along unfamiliar paths I will guide them; I will turn the darkness into light before them and make the rough places smooth. These are the things I will do; I will not forsake them. (Isaiah 42: 16)

In their case the god of this world has blinded the minds of the believers, to keep them from seeing the light of the gospel of the glory of Christ, who is the image of God. (2 Corinthians 4;4)

Jesus said, for judgment I came into this world, that those who do not see may see, and those who see may become blind. (John 9: 39)

The spirit of the Lord is upon me, because he has anointed me to proclaim good news to the poor. He has sent me to proclaim liberty to the captives and the recovering of sight to the blind, to set at liberty those who are oppressed. (Luke 4:18)

But whoever hates his brother is in darkness and walks in darkness, and does not know where he is going, because the darkness has blinded him. (1 John 2:11)

The Lord opens the eyes of the blind. The Lord lifts those who are bowed down; the Lord loves the righteous. (Psalms 146:8)

Inability to see as an African American life group

"And Jabez called on the God of Israel saying, 'oh, that you would bless me indeed, and enlarge my territory, that your hand would be with me, and that you would keep me from evil, that I may not cause pain.

(1 Chronicles 4:10)

There is neither Jew nor Gentile, neither slave or free, nor is there male and female, for you are all one in Christ Jesus.

(Galatians 3:28)

One of the problems in our society today is the devaluation of humanity within the eyes of one another. Let us examine the above scriptures. In Galatians Jesus dealt with three important categories that causes division in the world and in the church.

- *Jesus ended cultural distinction and separation by saying neither Jew nor Gentile*
- *Christ dealt with economic status and the exclusion of viewing people as individual property*
- *Gender preference and superiority due to gender and sexuality is canceled out by Christ*

Our Lord and savior states that we are one in unity, solidarity, purpose, application, and love through His character, authority, and spirit.

In the prayer of Jabez the Lord is articulating His agreement with man's need to expand his territory of reaching his fellow brothers and sisters in the earth with the gospel of Christ and through the application of love for thy neighbor.

It is critical that we notice that in this scripture of 1 Chronicles 4:10 that the request of Jabez was seeking how to treat people without causing pain and doing evil.

Our vision must be as men to create environments that allows us to fellowship and honor each other as God's life group upon the earth that are created to live and love as His children.

Woman

And God created them male and female and He called their name Adam. (Genesis 5:2)

It is imperative as men that we see women correctly. God created women in His image and likeness.

Women are the Father's daughters by relationship, and queens by position in His kingdom. The Lord created women as helpers to fulfill the vision implanted into men. A woman has the same holy spirit that we have. She is not inferior nor less than men in intellectual capacity, or worth. When the Bible states that women are the weaker vessel, the definition for weaker is delicate. Therefore, God is telling us to handle women with specialty. Gender is distinct roles. Women are nurturers, and mother's, they are designed by God to birth what is implanted within them both spiritually and physically.

When we see women as female dogs, gold diggers, loose sexually, or unworthy of marriage but good enough to sleep with, we are devaluing their essence and treating them less than how they were created to be loved.

Baby momma titles are the result of broken concepts of a relationship.

A woman who have birthed a man's child is the highest honor given to him by a her. A child is an extension of himself and an heir to carry on his bloodline. How we see women is vitally important to how we function in the church, world, and within our family. Let us look at a few key scriptures dealing with how our Lord views women.

"God is in the midst of her; she shall not be moved; God will help her when morning dawns. (Psalms 46:5)

"Charm is deceitful, and beauty is vain, but a woman who fears the Lord is to be praised. (Proverbs 31:10)

"I praise you, for I am fearfully and wonderfully made. Wonderful are your works; my soul knows it very well". (Psalms 139:14)

"Nevertheless, in the Lord woman is not independent of man nor man of woman; "for as woman is of the man, even so is the man also of the woman, but all things of God." (1 Corinthians 11-12)

"Do not let your adorning be external, the braiding of hair and the putting on of gold jewelry, or the clothing you wear, but let your adorning be the hidden person of the heart with the imperishable beauty of a gentle and quiet spirit, which in God's sight is very precious. (1 Peter 3: 3-4)

Marriage

The holy union between man and woman is the design of God. The earth was meant to be populated by children who were reared in a nuclear or a two - parent household that raised them in the admonition and love of God.

Marriage is the love of two people who have the desire and spiritual capacity to be life partners in both storms and sunshine. How we view marriage will determine how we treat the woman that we made vows to honor. Our word should be as God's. Our oath is one for eternity. In marriage we stood up before God and man and proclaimed, not until death shall we part, which means divorce is not on the table.

We must see marriage as the final choice of who I give my heart, body, soul, and life to. From that decision as a foundation we can now build a special and unique friendship, quality intimacy, and the process of forever enjoying and exploring seasons of mature and healthy lovemaking.

Marriage is not giving up being able to sleep with the assorted flavors of women and missing out on the spice of life as an alpha male. Marriage is maturity mating with the divine purpose of God and honoring his wife as the love of a lifetime and the best of promises and blessings that was given to him by God as his personal glory.

"A man should not have his head covered, because he is the image and glory of God; but the woman is man's glory. (1 Corinthians 11:7)

Relationships

Men must change how we view relationships with women. Firstly, we must learn to enter the introduction phase without having a sexual motive. Secondly, we must cease from thinking that all women are to be either girlfriends, one-night stands, or future wives, Thirdly, we must see women as social counterparts that are intricate values, and productive intellectuals, that serve and are served in the capacity of loving humanity and the sharing of goals, aspirations, and commonality. As men it is wise to have healthy relationships with all people.

A relationship with women should also be one that is known to the woman in your life. It should never be silent, hidden, and it should never be a replacement for a wife or fiancé when things do not go well.

A woman should never be a man's best friend when he is in a marriage. You should never be more comfortable telling another woman what you feel, juxtaposed to sharing your feelings with the woman who you love, cherish, honor, respect, and sleep with every night as the mother of your children or as the birth place of your love heart to heart.

As men we must keep in perspective the limits of men and women relationships. Bonds with women must stay non- sexual in content. They must be spiritually fruitful in nature. They must be healthy in application. And they must be pure in intentions. "That every one of you should know how to possess his vessel in sanctification and honor." (1 Thessalonians 4:4)

CHAPTER SIXTEEN

MENTAL PICTURE

Sex and making love are both physical expressions of a spiritual truth.

- Sex is the physical expression of lust and fornication that is ungodly in nature. It is concerned only with personal pleasure and takes no account for consequences, or the care and responsibility of birthing a child. Sex disregards God's word and is selfish in need and gratification. Sex is non- committal and a promiscuous risk for sexually transmitted diseases.
- Making love is a physical expression of a spiritual truth that is Godly in purpose.

Marriage is a holy institution and a scared place of confined fire that blazes in intensity that is blessed and ordained of God. Such pleasure is also found within the trust and learning of one another in ways that continue throughout a lifetime of intimacy, bliss, ecstasy, exploring and sharing the best that love can express while becoming one in all areas of human bond and friendship. "Marriage is honorable to all, the marriage bed is undefiled, but whoremongers and fornicators I shall judge" (Hebrew 13:4)

As I look out into the world, what I see is a need for the love of God to permeate throughout each relationship upon the earth. There is not a single person who should be exempt from experiencing the beautiful nature of who our Lord and Savior is as a person.

The most alluring picture that I can imagine is the world living as one big diverse family happily sharing their gifts, talents, finances, intelligence, and love on a global basis. If that vision is too big for you, then start with your family and simply love them in a way that is second to none.

CHAPTER SEVENTEEN

THE POWER OF HEALING

Christine walked slowly down the corridors of the hospital. Standing by in the waiting room as she turned the corner were six family members. They were all present over the last few days. Christine thought about what she would tell her loved ones.

At the sight of Christine, a couple of the men stood with a look of hope and expectancy upon their face. After all, this was John Hopkins, the best doctors that money could buy treated people here. The rich and affluent hung their faith on the skills and talents of the well learned, and upon the brightest minds in America when it comes to the medical profession.

Stephen was the first to speak.

"Chrissy, how is she?"

Immediately, by the look that shaded her aura, she did not need to voice the obvious. The family began to weep, one by one. Death had come to visit where there was no faith. Has COVID 19 found a faithless generation?

> **"Jesus called His twelve disciples together and gave them authority to cast out evil spirits and to heal every kind of disease and illness."**
>
> **(Matthew 10:1)**

My wife's mother Blanche Floyd, who I also love dearly as my mother. She once told me something I will never forget when I first began to preach in 2009. She told me that I can never preach about a faith that I do not have, and I cannot preach about a Jesus that I do not know. The revelation to her words of wisdom is this. As a Pastor I can preach about the Jesus that I read about and have heard about.

I can also preach about what Jesus said He can do because I believe it is true. Yet, I would not be preaching through existential knowledge, which is personal experience. Therefore, I would be preaching that Jesus heals, without knowing Him as a healer, because He has never healed me. Therefore, what kind of teacher would I be to teach about healing faith that I have not been a recipient of?

I have been in many churches, and I have heard uncountable sermons through television ministry

I have heard major preachers, who are world renown, teach unbiblical truths. It is dangerous when you do not study the word for yourself.

I have heard these television evangelists teach that God does not heal anymore. Certain pastors teach that healing stopped with the acts of the apostles.

Yet, the truth is, God is a God of clarity not confusion. Today, unfortunately you have millions of Christians who accept sickness and disease as a way of life. People across the globe are accepting something that they have power over.

One day I severely injured my left foot. I broke two bones and had three tears in the structure. Another time I blew out my knee and wounded my back. And each time, I prayed and was healed. Today, I know what my mom, Blanche Floyd, was saying those many years ago. Today, I can teach that Jesus heals because I personally know Him as a healer.

Today, I have faith that nothing is too hard for God because Of the many things that He has done for me that could not have been achieved by medicine or carried out by anything else. *You can have faith in the Bible because you believe what you are reading. However, you cannot know the Bible is true until you live it, and experience God for yourself.*

Dear people of God, let us examine a few scriptures that will testify to this truth that healing is the will of God.

I have learned to search the word for myself, so that I will know what God has said, and what He still speaks today. I do not serve a historical Jesus. I serve the living Jesus who sits on the right hand of the Father forever making intercession in the heavenly sanctuary at this present moment!

John 17:17 states that the word of God is truth. So, if we study the Bible then we can have faith that the words we read are indeed truth. The Bible reveals to us key occurrences that will change our lives in the area of sickness and disease. Saints of God, if you apply what is about to be revealed, your family, friends, and yourself can be saved from the fatal attack of the enemy.

Demonstration of Healing

- ➢ Matthew 9: 20-22; The woman with an issue of blood was healed after twelve years of being sick, after having spent all her money and after having seen many physicians
- ➢ Luke 17:11-19; Ten lepers were healed from an incurable disease that effects the nerves and respiratory tract.
- ➢ Mark 10: 46-52; Blind Bartimaeus was healed from Retinitis Pigmentosa, or Macular Degeneration.
- ➢ Mark 3:1-6; Jesus heals the man with the withered hand which was a result of poor circulation of blood, long disuse of the hand, or a deformity inherited from birth
- ➢ Matthew 9: 18-26; Jesus raised Jairus' daughter from the dead.

The above scriptures are evidence that Jesus heals.

"Jesus Christ is the same yesterday, and today and forever." (Hebrew 13:8)

"I am the Lord, I change not." (Malachi 3:6)

"Then Peter opened his mouth, and said, of a truth I perceive that God is no respecter of persons." (Acts 10: 34-43)

People of the living God, we have just viewed from the above scriptures that Jesus does not change. Which means that whatever He did two thousand years ago; He will do today. Also, the above text says that Christ is not a respecter of persons, meaning He does not show favoritism. Please take note of this vital point. **No one is blessed because they deserve it.** We are not blessed by works; we are blessed by position, by whom we are in Christ Jesus.

> **"For you died (To the control of sin) and your life is now hidden with Christ in God."**
> **(Colossians 3:3)**

It is vitally important that we understand this Biblical truth. The children of God have an inheritance. We are in a holy covenant with the Father through Christ Jesus. Therefore, we have direct access to every blessing possible from heaven.

Hebrew 4:16 tells us that we can approach the throne boldly, which means that we can enter into His holy presence with confidence, knowing that we will find, obtain, and receive what we need.

As we study the word of God, it informs us of our spiritual right to be healed, to prosper, and our right to inherit whatever Christ has been given by the Father. "His divine power hath given unto us all things that pertain unto life and godliness, through the knowledge of Him that hath called us to glory and virtue." (2 Peter 1:3)

"For those who are led by the spirit of God are the children of God, and if a son then a co-heir with Christ Jesus." (Romans 8;14)

<u>You can be healed today</u>

The year 2020 has been a very trying year for millions of people. COVID 19 has taken the lives of many. However, this is not the only disease that is killing people globally. Cancer, lupus, leukemia, H.I.V. Aids, and many other maladies, plagues, and human ills are wiping out large numbers of the population.

I do not believe that Jesus came to earth just to exonerate man from his sins, and to grant him everlasting life in heaven.

The Messiah also came to show us by example of how we should live, and how we should respond to what happens to us in life. He also came to leave us an inheritance. Ecclesiastes 1:9 tells us that there is nothing new beneath the sun.

In my personal studies I has discovered that COVID 19 carries many of the same attributes as leprosy, also known as Hansen's disease. Let us look at these amazing similarities, which I believe are the same strain of COVID 19. Leprosy affects the mucous membranes, within the inner lining of the nose, and the respiratory system.

Today, leprosy is contained to Africa and Asia. Asia is said to be where COVID 19 originated. Listen to this. Leprosy is transmitted via droplets from the nose and mouth. Another important key is found in how the people who had Leprosy had to conduct themselves.

Their hands and arms were covered, and masks to prevent the human contagion. In Biblical times the leper was sent to colonies which is being quarantined. This was a law, which we are seeing being conducted in the world today. We must wear mask to shop, and in some places like restaurants we must wear gloves and a mask when getting food from the buffet.

How did Christ deal with this sickness when He walked the earth? Jesus was unafraid of being contracted with the disease. Why is His actions different than ours today? Jesus knew His authority over leprosy.

"As He (Jesus) was going into a village, ten men who had leprosy met him. They stood at a distance (social distancing) and called out in a loud voice, "Jesus, Master, have pity on us!"

The word says that the ten were cleansed. The word cleansed carries this definition; A process or period during which a person rids the body of substances regarded as toxic or unhealthy.

"For He had healed many, so that those with diseases were pushing forward to touch Him." (Mark 3:10)

In Matthew 6:8 the Bible tells us that Jesus commanded that the Father's will in heaven be done or lived out upon the earth. Therefore, we can clearly see that Jesus healed the sick. We can also conclude that Jesus heals from the book of Revelation 22:2 whereas the word says that the tree of life (Symbolic of Jesus) bore fruit for the healing of the nations. This same truth is validated in Revelation 21: 4 "And God shall wipe away all tears from their eyes, and there shall be no more death, neither sorrow, nor crying, neither shall there be any more pain; for the former things have passed away.

Sickness and disease cause death. Sickness, poverty, disease, and death are a result of sin which comes from Satan. It is not God's will for us to be sick. Therefore, the people brought the sick and diseased to Christ and He healed them. Jesus is conducting the Father's will from heaven here upon the earth as told in Matthew 6:8. We are called to do the same things as Jesus.

Ephesians 5:1 says to be imitators of God. I believe that the church has failed in its call during this pandemic.

We are told to lay hands on the sick and they shall recover. Christ was not afraid of Simon the leper. He healed those with leprosy that has the same symptoms and characteristics as COVID 19.

"Lay hands on the sick, and they shall recover" (Mark 16:15)

This is the gospel or good news that Christ sent us to preach. That by His stripes we are healed. We have the power to alleviate the suffering of sickness and disease through the power of the Holy Spirit.

Saints of God, we do not have to accept what is not of God! We can live a healthy life, in addition to a loving and joyous life. Faith, application of the word, and obedience is always the key to victory.

CHAPTER EIGHTEEN

THE GOOD SAMARITAN

Before I venture into this familiar passage of scripture, I would like to articulate a point. We have just covered the vast topic of healing.

It is imperative that we couple healing with human treatment. A trained and skilled doctor can treat physical conditions, in much the same way that psychiatrist deal with mental issues. However, both situations of the mentally ill or the physically sick need a response to their condition by someone who is skilled, qualified, adapt, and willing. If we are to heal from the many issues that plague us as a nation of people, we will need those who are both willing and equipped with the heart of love for their neighbor. We must care about one another.

Most people with daycare centers care about children. People who care about their marriage and would like to remain married after a rough spot, would seek marriage counselors to refocus, refresh, restore, and move past certain issues. Therefore, until we learn to genuinely care for others, we cannot improve who we are as a person, nation, business, marriage, or as a church.

Personally speaking, I believe that certain problems can only be solved one way. I have been in many bad spots sort of speak. I have tried to cope with many problems by smoking cigarettes to calm my nerves, or I used marijuana to escape. At other times I turned to alcohol to numb my reality, or I tried sex to feel alive in insecure moments and a need of self-validation. I cannot count the times I used drugs to simply forget what is happening around me. Yet, none of it worked.

I had to evolve in the truth that God cares about me. I had to trust and realize that Jesus died for all of creation. His wish is that none should perish. This gift of eternal life is found within His work on the cross. However, before His death upon the cross, Jesus came only to the lost sheep of Israel. He came to open their eyes to their fallen state of salvation.

Yet, when He encountered those who were sick, poor, hungry, mentally disturbed, demon possess, or simply unlearned, He responded to their need because of love. He saw my need and was moved by compassion. *see (Matthew 9:36)

<u>Adopting the Spirit of Christ</u>

I was raised and told to respect authority figures, obey my elders, and do not talk to strangers.

If I experienced any trouble as a child, I was told to call the police. Growing up, I was told that the most trusted people in society at that time were the clergy, police, and schoolteachers.

➤ The clergy were entrusted with the spiritual development and guidance of our children.
➤ The police, were said to be trusted public servants who were sworn by duty to serve and protect the citizens in their community, while also upholding the law that they are sworn to protect.
➤ Teachers, are an exclusive brand of people who are entrusted with educating, shaping, and directing young minds toward careers, positive lifestyles, and proper beliefs in respect to how we behave through social norms in the interaction of people.

In 2020, our crisis is this; the people that we are supposed to trust and turn toward in a time of need are on very shaky ground morally.

For many years now, we have had unconscionable statistics of children being sexually abused by clergy in the Catholic Church.

We have experienced in recent years the high elevation of police brutality among blacks in our urban communities.

In our courtrooms across America, in a plethora of cases there has been evidence of perjury, falsified evidence, and unlawful incarceration of innocent men who were later freed from death row after serving twenty, twenty-five, and thirty years.

Unfortunately, in a lot of cases that are noncriminal, especially in urban cities, dealing with at risk children, alternative schools, or marginalized children who are impoverished for a variety of reasons, these minority children are overlooked.

In some of our urban areas, schoolteachers have become desensitized or lackadaisical in their approach to education, whereby, they work for a paycheck, or their mindset carries the attitude that hey, I am only here until something better comes along.

Although many may feel that child rearing is solely the role of the parent. I disagree. If I am wrong, why do we utter the words it takes a village, each one teaches one, leave no child behind, or we are a community of people? African American children need help! Outside of cancelled free lunch programs, poverty, a lack of updated computers and apps that parochial schools, private schools, Catholic schools, Montessori schools and charter schools are blessed with, city schools have other trying issues.

Within our school system it is not uncommon for teachers to have relationships with their students. According to my qualitative study in diverse demographics. One out of every ten students suffer abuse from a teacher or have experienced an inappropriate affair. One teacher can be responsible for up to 73 violations before they are caught according to the GAO (Government Accountability Office) report. My study focused upon young people, K-12. My information was gathered from the lessons that I learned from the title IX policy implementation of sexually abused students in America's school system.

Often schoolteachers who have relations with a student are passed off to three schools before the police are called in. It is a practice called "Passing the trash"

According to Wikipedia in 2020, 81% of students experience sexual harassment in school, 83% of girls have been harassed, and 38% were harassed by teachers. This is a crisis that few are dealing with. Another concern that I feel I must address is the practice of doping in urban schools.

Students across America are heavily medicated on the drug Ritalin.

This potent drug is dispensed to young children who has been said to be diagnosed for Attention-Deficit Hyperactivity Disorder. This potent drug alongside many other pathologies that minorities are diagnosed with in our school system, allows young children to become hooked on schedule

II drugs which are in the category of cocaine, heroin, methamphetamine, Adderall, Dextroamphetamine, Vyvanse, and other deadly drugs that are legal but considered dangerous because of their high risk of abuse and dependence. People of God ask yourselves. what happens when these young adults who have been taught to cope with life on these potent drugs are no longer in school? Who pays for the drugs? Sadly enough, a high percentage of these kids will turn to illegal drugs to cope with problems and their addiction, which sets the stage for crime, and mass incarceration. These actions are the premeditated genocide of young black males.

There are currently 1.4 million black men in college, juxtaposed to 840,000 black men in America's prison system.

I understand that many people may feel as though this is not their problem. However, corrupt police, perverted clergy, deviate teachers, mass incarceration, and drug induced students is a national crisis. So, how can we as a nation effectively deal with it? The answers are discovered in the story of the good Samaritan in Luke 10: 30-37.

Within this narrative there was a man who was severely beaten, robbed, stripped of his clothing, and left for dead. A priest while traveling came upon this gravely wounded man.

Yet, he did not help him in any way. He crossed over to the other side of the street as if nothing were wrong. Moments later, a Levite of the renowned priesthood from the chosen people of God looked upon the same wounded man who was fighting for his life and did nothing. The next person who came along in this captivating story was a Samaritan. The first thing that intrigued me about this parable, Was this. Why does God tell us the occupation of the first two men, but identify the next person by his culture?

"The real identity of a person is seen in how they reflect the image of God"

A Samaritan was a culture of people whom the Jews had declared as an unrighteous and unclean people.

These people dwelled in the ancient Palestine. As we get back to this story, the Samaritan stopped when he discovered the wounded man lying on the ground.

The Samaritan looked down at the man and saw his neighbor. He saw humanity, he looked at God's creation face to face, lying in the street alone, like an unloved and cast away dog.

The Samaritan responded to the need of the wounded with the heart of compassion, empathy, goodwill, and love for his fellow man.

The Samaritan's response was in the spirit of Jesus. He did everything within his power to do. He bound his wounds, poured oil over his cuts, and used wine to sterilize his injuries, and to prevent infection.

In addition to these lifesaving procedures, the Samaritan made financial provision for this stranger. The wounded man was carried to a place where he could rest, recuperate, and heal. In addition to the immediate needs of the wounded man, the Samaritan's act of kindness instructed the inn keeper to charge to his account any future expense.

As I think about Jesus the God of the oppressed, the Christological question that was raised within this terrific book that was written by James Cone, is this.

How does the Jesus who freed the Egyptians, who healed the sick, raised the dead, fed the poor, and defended His children against evil kings, relate to us today? Biblical truth must not relegate to just reciting historical events, the truth about Christ must be realized in our daily lives as proof of His activity.

My brothers and sisters we never know from where our help will come. God will always send aid in a time of need. Our crisis as African American people is found within this parable of the good Samaritan.

As a race of people, we find it hard to count on and depend on those who are not black. We do not trust those who are in a valid position to help due to skin color, or due to what those in that occupation has done before. As we evaluate the crisis of this parable, you will discover that the crisis was not the wounded man lying on the side of the road.

In many urban cities, robbery and crime is a major problem. Black on black victimization is a serious thorn in the sides of our growth and development as a culture. Yes, violence in our communities, and the fear of gang retaliation, has caused people to see the wounded and cross over to the other side of the street, acting identical to what the two priests did when they discovered the hurt man in the story of the good Samaritan. However, crime and violence are a grave issue in urban cities.

The greater tragedy, and misfortune occurs, when you study this parable and figure out that both men that passed by this severely wounded man were priest.

When people of God do nothing in response to human suffering, we have failed in our call from Him to love thy neighbor, as we love Him.

We also have failed to be effective in a person's life when we were able and equipped to do so but did nothing.

It is the vocation of these priest to be spiritual leaders, to attend to hurting, and broken people. It is the priest duties to care for God's creation, to minister to the ills of people, to counsel, to wed, to comfort at funerals, to baptize, to christen babies, and to be a pillar in their community through outreach programs for America's poor and disabled.

So, the question is. With the sacred trust that is given to these priests, why did both leave a wounded man lying on the ground, stripped of his clothing, robbed of his possessions, and defrauded of his right to be healthy? To understand the why is crucial as it pertains to the problems that we face as African Americans here upon the shores of America.

Firstly, why would both priests go and look at the wounded man and then do nothing once they discovered his identity, even though he was severely wounded?

➢ Both priests realized that the man was not a part of their congregation
➢ He was a different culture or ethnicity
➢ Neither priest could receive anything from helping the man. It would cost them something, time, money, inconvenience, and the giving of themselves as a loving person

Being a priest or a pastor must be more than a paycheck, or tithes and offerings. This call from God must respond to the service of human need. Jesus said, "I came not to be served but to serve." (Matthew 20:28)

Our crisis today is that we disregard people based upon their social status, religious affiliation, political party, financial ability, or race. As a culture we are failing drastically at responding to human need. When we gaze at struggling black folks, many times we act just like the two priest who ignored the wounded man lying on the road of need. We often weigh the cost of our attention, time, involvement, money, and then abandon the human need because of the person who needs help is not our friend, or family.

The challenge of 2020 and 2021 amid the ravishes of COVID 19 is how will we respond to the conditions of our society regardless of kindred connection? It is a massive need that we respond to our human connection, understanding that we are our brother's keeper. However, before we can respond with love, we must believe that all people are created equal, and are worthy of common courtesy, dignity, and respect. To abort evil and birth change, we must respond with who we are as Christians, functioning as many members but one body of priest.

The man who was a Samaritan and whom the Jewish church viewed as unclean responded to the hurt and wounded while the church leaders of the priesthood dishonored their vocation and God by doing nothing.

If you were laying in the street wounded, naked, bleeding, robbed, and in the throes of death, wouldn't you want someone to help?

The good Samaritan is a scathing formal accusation upon America.

If we are a noble people, we must meet the needs of our brethren, regardless of race, culture, or creed.

> **"Every person that is restored to health, that person can now make healthy choices that will impact another person's life with a healthy experience"**

CHAPTER NINETEEN

FATHERHOOD, MENTORS, AND LEADERS

Allured by the blaring noise and the colorful lights flashing from the police sirens, Terrance was drawn to his living room window. Thoughts of his father gave life to the last time that he had seen him. Looking at the police cars, Terrance wondered if at this moment was his father being chased, or beaten by the mean men wearing blue uniforms, who carried those big ugly sticks that wacked brothers upside the head.

Charles came into the room.

"Time to go to bed, little man."

Irate at having the thoughts of his dad interrupted, Terrance turned around with a menacing scowl upon his face.

"You aren't my father!"

Charles took a deep breath before he spoke softly in response to Terrance's outburst.

"I may not be the man who fathered you, but it takes more than sleeping with your mother to be a man. I raised you and gave you a second chance. I married your mom, adopted you, gave you a lovely home, and was there for you during the roughest moments in your life. You may not understand it now, but I love you and I only want what is best for you. However, you have to want what is best for yourself."

42% of black preschoolers are suspended from school, 26% of black children are in foster care, instead of being in nuclear families. Due to single parenthood the average black households net worth is $ 6,446.00 with an average of $ 34,598 a year to support a family of four. African American's have experienced 194 billion dollars in losses through home foreclosure.

56% of victims injured by police are black men due to their criminal activities. Only 5.4% of black males are a part of the rising economy verses 10.1 % of black women. And 10 % of blacks receive social security due to how few have ever worked legal jobs. Blacks are victims of predatory lending practices by banks at an alarming 63%.

While 39% of black owned businesses folded during 2014 and is much higher during COVID 19, 12.2 % of blacks were discriminated upon regarding medical treatment in 2015. During this pandemic, the numbers are much higher.

We see that 71% of Afro-American women are raising their children without their biological fathers in the home. Most of these women are forced to work two jobs or go to school and work just to make ends meet. Many problems in our society can be traced to a lack of fatherhood, leadership, and mentors. When I was growing up one of the things that I never saw, was a man of God. Every man that I knew was a hustler, cheater, and lived according to the code of the streets. The mentors that I had in the city of Detroit, were pimps, players, drug dealers, and gang leaders.

A lot of young men face the same problem that I had when I was growing up. Many men who hustle or who find themselves behind bars ask the following inquiries.

➢ Who was there in my life to show me how to be a man?
➢ Who was there on a consistent basis with love and concern?

➢ Who was there to display an example of maturity as it pertains to how a man treats a woman?

➢ Who was there to depict how a man earns a living for his family without breaking the law?

➢ Who was there to reflect who God is in our home?

➢ Who was there to teach a promiscuous man monogamy?

If we as a culture are to reach this generation of un-fathered youth, I believe we need to understand the dynamics of what happened with the first recorded broken family on the earth, which is depicted in the book of Genesis, chapter one through four. Although Adam and Eve did not get divorced after Adam disobeyed God and caused his family to be evicted from the Lord's presence, which held all their blessings and earthly provision. A tragedy did happen. Man's reality has become living in a sinful state of being instead of living in the comfort and eternal blessings of a holy institution.

Man was severely wounded through the brokenness of fatherhood.

The broken link between Adam and his spiritual Father transferred into the life of his sons. His first-born son Cain, inherited the propensities of Adam, which came from the spiritual nature of Satan whom they chose to follow instead of the path that God had already laid out for them. Let us evaluate the dialogue between God and Cain and you will see the attitude of the adversary which opposes the will of submission to God's righteousness.

The story begins here in (Genesis 4:6-16)

6) "And the Lord said unto Cain, why art thou wroth (angry) and why is thy countenance (acceptance and favor of God) fallen?

7) "If thou do well, shalt thou not be accepted? And if thou do not well, sin lieth at the door and unto thee shall be his (Satan's) desire, and thou shalt rule over him (Satan)." ***If you take dominion over him!***

Cain disobeyed God and refused to bring the right sacrifice and thus according to verse 16, he was sent from the Lord's presence to dwell in the land of Nod, on the east of Eden.

At this juncture it is particularly important to define what the land of Nod stands for. By definition it means a place of wandering. Which means that as a young man Cain is wandering aimlessly from place to place in life without his earthly father Adam, and without his spiritual Father God.

This is the problem with today's youth. When young men do not have proper male examples, mentors, guidance, and spiritual compasses, they are often doomed to pattern after lyrics in a rap song, after immature males, irresponsible males, violent thinking males, criminal minded males, and ungodly males. In most cases although these types of males have detrimental character defects, they are often disguised by tough bravado, violent street cred, flashy cars, money, and beautiful women. Therefore, the unlearned of God and the misled, will be impressed and indoctrinated by a false sense of manhood and fall into a trap that usually leads to an early grave, a drug rehab, or the penitentiary.

"There are no short cuts to being a man."

Jesus is the pattern son for all of humanity as it relates to living as an example of His Father. However, knowing this truth is different than applying this truth.

Performance Matters

To perform means to fulfill, to function, to carry out instructions, or to do a task in a set manner. Young men without proper leadership will often encounter problems because they have never learned to submit or surrender to a voice they respect, or they have failed to recognize the character in a man that they admire and wish to emulate.

The Bible teachers us that faith without works is dead. Meaning, we have to perform certain duties, which is designed to enjoin with what God is doing for things to work out for our good. However, a person who does not like to listen, who does not like authority, or seem to always know a better way, or it's their way or the highway will be bad performers. (i.e.) If an actor or actress cannot perform on stage according to the script...but is great while performing at home in the mirror, doing it their way.

What good is that? Their in-house act is irrelevant. The paycheck comes from performing when it counts.

Being able to fulfill the contract, carry out instructions, or being able to function under pressure and in clutch moments matters in life. Success and failure often hinge upon how prepared we are for the particular task.

Life, children, and women put pressure on men to perform their duties of adulthood. Men do not make excuses they make adjustments. It is vitally important that young men are taught what is expected of them within a committed relationship, marriage, as head of the household, and in the workforce. Jesus said it this way. Can a man build a house and not consider the cost?

Dr. Miles Monroe said:" It is dangerous to do a dreadful thing well." Too many black men are making huge sums of cash by committing crime in the streets. Therefore, the subculture that they have created that says we don't need to live by the culture of America and the white man's way of life, is destroying a generation of young men who think they can get rich by selling drugs, and identity theft.

If we are to be successful as men, loving leaders of our family, effective voices in our community, in the church, on the job, and in politics, we must man up and accept responsibility for both our actions and lack of actions.

Successful people learn how to be punctual; they know how to obey or follow instructions even if they do not agree with the procedure of what is being done. I remember one day I was at work doing a job in a lady's home. Me and my boss Greg was laying ceramic tile. Greg asked me to perform a certain task and I said well I think it would work better if we did it this way. My boss said something that I will never forget. He said. "I don't pay you to think. I pay you to do what I ask you to do. If something goes wrong on this job, I am the one who has to give this lady back over ten thousand dollars."

As men we were created to be fruitful. Our Creator, our heavenly Father wishes that we have life and life more abundantly. However, to obtain this promise, we must perform as a seed that becomes a larger harvest of its own kind. Meaning we must emulate the God that we came from.

CHAPTER TWENTY

HOW TO BE PRODUCTIVE

A farmer does not plant seeds in frozen ground. Why not? He understands that it would be futile, out of season and unfruitful. He also understands that his valuable seed would be wasted. Therefore, even though a farmer is prepared to sow, has the proper seed, cleared out land, and the right tools for the job, he must still wait for other factors to take place before he can successfully launch into his plans, and enjoy the endeavors of a rich and plentiful harvest that will feed his family, and allow him to sell his produce to earn a decent living and gather future savings.

One of the factors that the farmer must wait for that is equal to being in the right season and having the right seed, is having the **soil broken** to receive seed. (This can refer to the heart) Secondly, the farmer needs to **cultivate** the garden and keep the **weeds** out. (This can refer to people and things that hinder your growth)

Thirdly, he must **trust** God to bring both the right amount of sunshine, and rain (Surrender to God's will) to birth increase. After this task and function. The farmer must become a salesperson, and a good businessperson. It would be prudent if the farmer knew how to deal with other people. We should not have a nasty attitude and expect people to be in a relationship with us, or to do business with us despite how we doggedly treat them.

Men, we also need to be good stewards over what we have been entrusted with. (Resources, networking, funding) The farmer's oats, grain, rice, and wheat must be delivered on time, and in excellent quality in order for him to align future sells and satisfy his clientele.

"Soldiers must perform well to win the war."

God is our Father. So, ask yourself what does it take for Him to be successful at raising us up as His son's?

- ➤ A strategy and workable plan
- ➤ Understanding of different temperament and patience
- ➤ A standard of set examples in fatherhood
- ➤ The love and willingness to be open and honest
- ➤ Unconditional grace mercy forgiveness and provision

For God to visit His people on earth, He had to create a workable plan for leaving a spiritual and holy environment to enter a physical sinful realm. ** Note* God did not change who is to carry out this truth.* He created a body whereas He could take on human flesh and become a sanctified example for us in this worldly system. God then created a way for man to fellowship with Him and to enter into His presence through spiritual laws. God had a prophet by the name of Moses build a sanctuary in a set manner that reflected His sanctuary in heaven. God met with man there.

Let us examine the traits of Jesus that allows men to see how we can raise our youth.

- ➤ He was willing to become like man to relate to man
- ➤ He was willing to make a personal investment in His fellow man
- ➤ He was willing to be of service to the needs of others
- ➤ He was willing to give His all to better His brethren
- ➤ He did not deviate from what His Father taught him even in the face of adversity and personal loss
- ➤ He was obedient to the instructions of the Father
- ➤ He displayed love in equality
- ➤ He did not break his promises and He kept his word

- ➢ He was a man worth following
- ➢ He was never selfish
- ➢ He always displayed compassion
- ➢ His lifestyle was a godly education in how to live
- ➢ He never failed to respond with love

As men we can learn from the performance of Jesus in how to be men and in how to be examples to today's youth.

Aristotle says that a youth who has received a good upbringing will enjoy acting virtuously. Youth, according to Aristotle, are enslaved to their desires. Each day they seek to gratify what their appetite for pleasure dictates. Aristotle further states in his thesis: No one is born with a moral compass. We learn-or not- from our upbringing.

That is why father's feel such great responsibility and are hurt and lash out when they fall short.

> "Jesus was raised in heavenly principles, which allowed Him to withstand earthly temptations."
>
> Pastor T. L. Hughes

CHAPTER TWENTY-ONE

THE POWER OF TRANSFORMATION

"Christ mission was understood by the people of His time. The manner of His coming was not in accordance with their expectations... this expectation Christ answered in the parable of the sower.

> Not by force of arms, not by violent interpositions, was the kingdom of God to prevail, but by the implanting of a new principle in the hearts of men."
>
> Ellen G. White

In order to thrive as a person, family, business, church, or as a nation of people there must be transformation. We cannot remain in this current state of human behavior and be happy, or successful. History has taught us many things, divorces, prior relationships, bankruptcy, poverty, poor living conditions, race relations, dead end jobs, sickness and false friendships has opened our eyes to a need for change, I have heard it said that the definition of insanity is to do the same thing and expect a different result. Jesus said, "Conform not to the world, but be ye' transformed through a renewal of the mind." (Romans 12:2)

Transformation is to change in structure, character, or appearance. COVID 19 has destroyed the structure of life, traditions, and how people are accustomed to doing things.

Many people after the Trump administration will have to mend broken relationships, damaged integrity, and divided churches.

Building the life that we want will take a solid structure. I personally believe that smart people should surround themselves with likeminded people who have built or have done successfully whatever you are currently striving to achieve. This will cut major mistakes and arm you with personal exposure to growth and development. Balance is the key. Success takes priority. As a race of negritude, Afrocentricity, and a regal culture who has been mistreated by so many people, we need to be good to ourselves in a meaningful and lasting manner.

> *"The carnal mind wants to shine in its carnality, and hide in its religiosity"*
>
> *Apostle Michael Scott*

Trust your instinct, recognize the difference between a hustle and a blessing. Be careful who you allow to lead you. Jesus said you will know my children by their fruit. If God has placed someone in your life, the reason will surface in enhancement, value, growth, prosperity, open doors, need, and answered prayer. Fruit is productivity in kingdom affairs, and righteous living. When Jesus enters a situation there's always transformation. Christ was both a visionary and a revolutionary.

> *"Transformation is seen in visual application"*

Let us evaluate this truth through a remarkable event that took place in the Bible. Upon a place called the Mount of Transfiguration Jesus transformed into the level of a spiritual being in order to communicate with those in the spirit realm. Jesus had a meeting on the earth with the prophet Moses and Elijah who had passed away many years ago. (Matthew 17:2)

What is God telling us here? The principle is this. In order to elevate to a higher calling, we must respond to that level of the word in obedience and understanding. Jesus could not talk to Moses and Elijah through His flesh because they are in the spirit. Therefore, spiritual things are discerned by spiritual things. We walk not by the flesh but by the spirit.

Moses and Elijah would not have been able to relate to Christ in the flesh. In the similitude that Christ transformed on the mount is the same way we are to transform the world with the culture of the kingdom of God. We, as a people, are to have conversations of faith not worldly communication that profits us nothing. Jesus transformed into what it took to receive counsel from the realm of the spirit.

Moses and Elijah had both dealt with stiff necked people and corrupt leaders, while Jesus had not yet met such men through existential occurrences. They were giving Him comfort and ministry.

For complete understanding, allow me to get a little more practical in terms of dealing with transformation. (i.e.) When going to a job interview, the person looking to receive the job must transform their appearance to fit the environment of the company. If you are a beautiful woman for instance. You may look great in a bathing suit. However, you cannot wear your bikini to a Fortune 500 Company. Yes, it looks great at the beach, but this is a different environment. A person should present him or herself as being one with the structure. Your appearance should suggest that you are in one accord with the company that you represent.

In John 17:21 Jesus said: "I pray that they become one with one another as we are one." We, as a people are, created to mirror on the earth the holy reflection of heaven in our dealings with one another. In order to succeed we must be able to transform. In order to handle information by revelation, and perform according to a specific purpose, it takes the power of reformation and the ability to transform. Yet, none of this is possible if we as a people, as father's, mother's, leaders, and mentors do not conform to the spirit and ideologies of success.

To conform means to be similar or identical, or to obey customs or a higher standard.

God warns us not to conform to a system that opposes, rejects, rebels against, and is contrary to His holiness, commandments, laws, precepts, statues, and ordinances. We cannot live in the kingdom like we lived in the world. We cannot act in the church the way we behaved in the bar.

A single person while single can live for themselves. However, once they get married, now their money is no longer their own. He or she must transform their thinking and conform to the laws of oneness in marriage by being monogamist, and living in a way that is always for "us" and not just "I."

When we are confronted with new challenges, trials, obstacles, and tribulations, please do not be in haste. Be wise and prudent. Be patient, make intelligent decisions, endure with grace, and learn from mistakes as you move forward knowing and believing that greater is He that is in you than he that is in the world. We can do all things through God who strengthens us.

CHAPTER TWENTY-TWO

IF YOU BELIEVE YOU RECEIVE

There is a story in the Bible where a man's daughter was very sick. The caretaker came to Jesus and asked Him to heal her. However, while they were on their journey, the young girl died. Having learned of this...

The person who had originally came to Jesus stopped Him on the road and said. "Why trouble the master any further. The damsel is dead". And Jesus turned to the parents who has authority over the young girl's life, and said "fear not, only believe" (Luke 8:50)

Abram was a man raised in an idolatrous household, yet when God came to him and told him that He would make him the father of many nations and would bless him above all men upon the earth and make his name famous. He believed God. And riches, and a baby was given to his barren wife. (James 2:23)

"Yet to all who did receive Him, to those who believed in His name, He gave the right to become children (Inheritors of all blessings) of God" (John 1:12)

In order to receive from the Father, you must believe in His word and in who Christ is as the savior of the world. The following text reveals a powerful truth. Matthew 18:18 says "whatsoever you bind on earth I shall bind in heaven, and whatsoever you lose on earth shall be loosed in heaven."

The Greek word for bind in the above text means this: I declare to be prohibited and unlawful. Example, if poverty or sickness attacks you...

God says according to Matthew 6:8 "Thy will shall be done on earth according to His will (word) as it is in heaven"

There is no sickness or poverty in heaven. Therefore, you can bind it, loose it, reject it, and not receive what the enemy has released upon your life. The Greek word for loose means to destroy, break, and dissolve the stronghold of what was prohibiting your blessings from God. Also * see Acts 21:11

Children fear not only believe and you will receive what the Lord has in store for you. * note Jesus said in John 11: 40: "Did I not tell you that if you believe, you will see the glory of God?" and they took away the stone and Lazarus came from the tomb.

CHAPTER TWENTY-THREE

THE KEYS TO FINANCIAL FREEDOM

I personally believe that this part of the Crisis and Challenges of Black America is most important outside of our relationship with Jesus Christ, our Lord and Savior. I say this because I understand that poverty is under the curse.

I also understand that money is a tool to invest in people, and the means by which we do the work of the kingdom as we take care of the poor, the widow, and the fatherless.

Renown Pastor R.A. Vernon said: "There's two things that the church always wants more of, but fear talking about, sex and money"

For many years we have experienced a split in the church of Christ due to many denominations being at odds with what has been coined the "Prosperity Gospel"

Name it and claim it shouts have run rapid in upbeat, lively, sanctified churches. Often, struggling churches feel that this gospel is false or else why aren't they blessed financially? Is money about how much faith you have? Is it about how many members you have? What about those who are Christians and are not pastors or ministers? Should they have money according to the Bible? I am a student of the word.

I am anointed to both teach and preach the gospel. I am honored and humbled to be assigned this arduous task. I am also an Africa American man. Therefore, I must bring this message to a culture of people that it will help most. I believe in a God of the oppressed. Though this Biblical truth is for all of God's children, I am making an intentional thrust at pushing this truth into the hearts, spirit, and mind of my people.

And so, allow me to present to you the uncompromised truth as it pertains to the matter of money according to God's word.

Wealth in America

"It is important that we monetize all of your gifts to create a beautiful symphony of income streams"
DR. Lynn Richardson

"One way to start to get control of your money is to spend less of it" If you live by the 10-10-30-50 rule. The first 10% you tithe, the next 10% you save, 30% is cash in your pocket for incidentals, and the remaining 50% is for your living expenses."
Dr. Lynn Richardson

Black income is half that of whites which is no different than it was in the 1950's. The wealth of the median black family in the U.S. has fallen to 10% of white counterparts. In 1953 four fifths of white families made more than the typical black family. According to the 2020 median, households of African American's average income is the lowest of all races at $30,134 per house, in comparison to Asian's at $85,349, whites at $ 67,865, Native Hawaiian and others at $ 50,987, and Hispanic earnings at $46,882 per household.

Regarding white collar jobs, blacks are usually marginalized due to the average income being listed as upper class at $57,617 annually. These jobs are also defined as opportunities that require a background check, drug screening, 2-5 years' experience, and an educational degree.

According to the census bureau the black household earned just 59 cents for every dollar white made. The average income for a two-family household in white America is $ 61,347 which according to the bureau of labor statistics amounts to $865 a week or $ 31,099 per person not per family. Most African American families fall into the basis statistic of poverty line status with an income of $22,314 for a family of four.

It is a fact that 93.6 million people fell below the poverty line, 28.9% are children living in poverty which by rate is 11.9 million, and 12.9% or 21.4 million of women of African American descent is in poverty.

Contributing factors for poverty

Among the enrolled students in school which is 84.6% amid blacks, 13% of our youth have dropped out of school, and only 45% attain high school diplomas. The gender wage gap between men and women is 3.8%, which is forty cents on the dollar. Another key factor that aids in the poverty of blacks is the teen birth rate that is at 18.8%.

As I studied these daunting statistics unemployed blacks before COVID 19 was at 27.4%. It's much higher today. Blacks are incarcerated at 4,347 per 100,000, while whites are jailed at 678 per 100,000, 44% of juveniles incarcerated are black.

The United States have locked up so many blacks that it has warped the negro reality. Unemployment for blacks rose from 7.65 in 2007 to 17.3 in 2010. However, during the Obama tenure though unemployment peaked at 10%, he brought it down to 4.7 % in 2016.

There are 2.6 million black owned businesses in America and 5.4 million are owned by whites. The 1 million two hundred thousand and sixteen newly started small businesses with paid employees are white owned. What I feel is the number one program in America that serves as a disincentive to work is the welfare system, or TANF which carry a staggering number of 110,489,000 people. 39% are blacks.

In 2020, blacks enrolled in college has fallen to 36% according to non HBCU Universities.

The above data is very troubling, but factual. Therefore, we must ask a Christological question. Do you believe that this is God's will for His children? Absolutely not! Therefore, let us now venture into the blessings of God and His design for money concerning the church and His children.

"Every healthy tree bears good fruit, but a diseased tree bears bad fruit."

(Matthew 7:17)

Stewardship in the regards to money is defined as responsible planning and management of resources provided by God for the betterment of creation. A steward is a person of trust. (Genesis 41:53-54)

The key to God's method of increase. is trusting the Lord with what you have and trusting God's word to produce what He promises. * SEE Malachi 3:8, 10,11, Deuteronomy 8:18, 28:8, Galatians 6:7, and Psalms 112: 1-5

It is imperative that we understand that God's plan for money is to support the function of the kingdom without lack, and to support the work of salvation. * See Matthew 6:10, Psalms 119:89,90, James 1:27, Genesis 12:2-3

At this time, I'd like to segue and talk about the five types of wealth in the kingdom and how they are applied. People of King Jesus, if you are obedient to these principles your entire life will change.

I am not giving you my opinion, I am giving you Scriptures for you to research and attach to your faith, so that you will be set free from the curse of poverty and debt. Later in this chapter I will give you the steps to debt cancelation and wealth increase.

Five Types of Wealth

- ➤ Sovereign wealth
- ➤ Transitional wealth
- ➤ Transformation wealth
- ➤ Wisdom wealth
- ➤ Relationship wealth

Sovereign wealth is money that is passed down directly from God. The Israelites did as Moses instructed and asked the Egyptians for articles of silver, gold and clothing, the Lord made the Egyptians favorably disposed toward the people and they gave them what they asked for. (Exodus 12: 35,36)

"And as I may so say, Levi also, who received tithes, payed tithes in Abraham. (Hebrew 7: 9) For those who may not grasp the above text. Abraham was the first person in the Bible to tithe. He gave to the priestly office of heaven which was symbolic of Christ. In return, God gave the increase (harvest) to him and his grandchildren the Levites.

In 1 Kings 17:13-14 an elderly woman was in lack and prepared to die. All she had left was a cake for her and her son.

However, the prophet asked the woman for the meal. She obeyed and received an abundance of meal that lasted until God sent rain and crops.

"The blessings of the Lord market rich and adds no sorrow." (Proverbs 10:22)

Transitional wealth is when you reap what you sow. This type of earning accrues from person to person, and through your job. The salvation army and the goodwill are prime examples of this wealth. They receive gifts from people, and they sell the clothes or gifts for financial gain. This is transitional wealth. When we obey the tithing principle in Malachi 3:8 God promises to bless your bank account (Storehouse) because you supplied money for His storehouse. The Lord shall command "*The Blessing" (money)upon thee in thy (your) storehouses,* and in all that thou set thine hand unto, and he shall bless thee in the land which the Lord thy God giveth thee (you) (Deuteronomy 28:8)

Remember this: There is a mentality of trust when you offer gifts to God. "Whoever sows sparingly will also reap sparingly, and whoever sows generously will reap generously." (2 Corinthians 9:6)

Transformation wealth is the wealth of the wicked that is stored up for the just. This money is designed to immediately change your life and financial situation.

"A good man leaves an inheritance for their children's children, but a sinner's wealth is stored up for the righteous." (Proverbs 13:22)

"I sent you to reap what you have not worked for, others have done the work, and you have reaped the benefits of their labor." (John 4:38)

We can see that God has a plan to change the poverty of His children. We need to understand that the fullness of the earth and everything in it belongs to God. Sinners are getting rich off the land that they do not have a covenant right to possess. The children of Israel when they departed Egypt left with the riches of the land. They were in bondage and poverty one night, but the blessings of God allowed them the next night, to wake up free and rich. They had so much money that when Moses took an offering to build the sanctuary of God, he had to tell them to stop giving. * See (Exodus 36:5)

As a race of people these keys are vital to turning our lives around. Most often when we are turned down for small business loans, and denied equal property bids, and low interest rates, we find ourselves scrambling to find another source of self-reliance. However, God's plan should be our first route to prosperity because He empowers us to be successful and full of fruit.

It is important that we grasp the concept of Psalm 1:3 which states: "He shall be like a tree planted by the river; he shall not be moved. He shall reap in due season, even in a time of famine his leaves shall not wither."

God is informing us that if we trust in His financial system that even when the world's economy dries up His children shall still flourish. King David said it this way. He has never seen the righteous forsaken nor beg for bread.

Wisdom of wealth is having the ability to produce fruit with God knowledge. God told Abraham; "I will make your name famous."

"Having a good name is wealth in currency."
Apostle Matthew Stevenson

A good name is priceless. People can be your greatest commodity in the arena of finances. The Proverbs 31 woman is wealthy through wisdom. She sees, saves, purchases, works diligently, and honors both God and her husband. She understands seasons and the purpose of money. "If any of you lack wisdom, you should ask God, who gives generously to all without finding fault, and it will be given you without reproach." (James 1:5)

As instructed in Deuteronomy 8:18, God gives us power (ability) to get wealth so that He can prove the covenant that He made with our ancestors.

In wisdom we must learn to partnership with covenant men in position to open doors and to fund your vision.

Most grants or the best grants occur when other people give you money for your dreams. This truth is realized in Habakkuk 2:2 when God says, "write the vision down and make it plain, and those who see it will run after it." In other words, people with money will fund your vision because they can see the value in what God has revealed through you.

The last category of wealth is relationship wealth. This is money that we are privy to due to who we are related to. In our case as Christians, we are sons of God, therefore we are co-heirs with Christ Jesus which affords us the opportunity to gain access to the wealth of heaven that is released in the earth to fulfill God's will for His Creation. (Romans 8:17)

We have covered Proverbs 13:22 whereas the children became rich due to the labor of the father. When we as God's children rest in the finished labor of Christ on the cross the same affect happens. (Mark 2:7)

"And Jesus came and said to them, "all authority in heaven and on earth has been given to me. "(Matthew 28:18-20)

Adam was given a land of gold in the book of Genesis. Gold was the sole form of currency from Biblical times until 1933. Jesus as a baby was given gold. Both were due to relationship. The father was supplying for Adam's future, and the Father was supplying for His Son's future as He hid in Egypt away from the death attempt of King Herod.

Before I venture into the mindset of money, and the warfare of wealth, allow me to first instruct us in how to get out of debt so we can be free to be a blessing to others.

CHAPTER TWENTY-FOUR

HOW TO DEAL WITH DEBT

"The rich rule over the poor, and the borrower is a slave to the lender."

(Proverbs 22:7)

We can see from the above text that the person who is in debt is a slave for a couple of reasons. (i.e.) the owner can repossess the car you owe money on, he can foreclose on the house you owe a mortgage on, the bank can raise the interest rates on your loan, and the government can garnish your wages for debt. Therefore, when you are in debt you have no control over the money that you earn. Other people dictate how you spend your money once you go against God's plan of stewardship and fall into the worlds system. Check and loan places, title car loan places, and high interest rate credit cards are all quick ways to get into debt that places you in financial bondage.

Here are the keys to erasing debt.

➢ Jesus said in Luke 14: 28 "Can a man build a house and not consider the cost?" Every dollar should have a name on it. (i.e.) If you have $50.00 earmarked for entertainment. Once you spend that money, do not go into the money that is for the light bill. Stick to the plan. If you want to get out of debt the first thing you need to do is to get a written 30-day budget and follow it monthly. Some months your money may fluctuate, so make adjustments according to what your income is for those thirty days. Make a list of your liabilities and your assets.

Your liabilities are what you owe out each month, and your assets is what you earn. Then figure out what gets paid and the order which you can pay down debt and stick to it.

➢ Your income is your biggest wealth building tool. Psalm 26:2 says the curse comes not without a cause. Meaning the curse of poverty doesn't just happen. We get into debt by poor budgeting, or no budgeting at all. We overspend and overextend ourselves. So, the key to cutting debt, or paying down debt is to get rid of credit cards, and stope buying things that you do not need.

➢ Foster high quality relationships. 1 Corinthians 15:33 informs us that filthy communication corrupts good manners.

Blessed are those who hunger and thirst after righteousness and they shall be filled. Talk to people at your bank about investment plans. Talk about ways to use your 401k, IRA, ROTH, or your portfolio. Learn how to diversify income. The bank has plans where they match what you invest and plans that even if you lose money you can never lose what you initially invest. You can always protect your money and obtain savings accounts that gain higher interest returns. Have a good relationship with people who handle your money it will go a long way.

➢ Save and invest. "Lord teach us to obey from a heart of love and gratitude; to hear your voice and respond in obedience," (Proverbs 21:20)

➢ Give to charity or church and the return principle will increase your life (Exodus 25: 31-38, 30: 7-8)

Steps to Erase Debt

Pay off debt from the smallest bills to the largest.

Budget monthly as detailed earlier in this chapter. Apply the 50/30/20/ rule. Place 50% of earnings toward living expenses. Save 30% tithe 10% and save 10% for walk around money.

Building success

Fire: Financial Independence Retire Early is a concept for erasing debt and saving the type of income that will allow you to retire early. The process is conducted by doubling payments that you owe.

This allows you to pay whatever you owe in half the allotted time. Things such as student loans, credit cards, car notes, and mortgages.

Ladies this tip is for you. Do not allow men to tell you this;" Oh, don't you worry your pretty little head about such things," as advised by psychologist Phyllis Chesler. In her eye-opening book, "Girl, Get Your Money Straight;" a sister's guide to healing your bank account and funding your dreams in 7 simple steps. Glinda Bridgforth recommends that women be smart, strong, and employable.

Ladies, a lot of men want you to be dependent upon them so they can control you and manipulate you through what they provide. However, I am not saying a man is not supposed to provide for you. I am saying a man's loving leadership is much different than being controlling and a premeditated hinderance to your personal dreams and aspirations that would afford you financial freedom.

Key principle: I must reiterate this point. Every dollar should have a name on it.

You should be able to break down your paycheck into sections. Needs, bills, food, savings, and wants is last. Retirement and old age come together. Both are a reality that you must prepare for.

If you are not comfortable with the 50/30/10/10 rule which is also supported by financial experts such as Dr. Lynn Richardson, Dave Ramsey, Tim Robbins, and Suze Orman, you can use this system; 50% of your earnings going toward groceries, rent, utilities, and your health, 30% going on dining out, hobbies, shopping, Netflix, and 20% going on savings, investments, and paying off debt. This is for those of you who do not tithe, although you cannot expect increase from God's system, as black people you must still have a plan. It's time to get serious about your future.

Let us look at the wisdom of God through what He instructed Adam to do. *Note* This is the prototype of our financial plan in the kingdom of heaven. In Genesis 1: 26-28 Adam was given five instructions. The first obligation was to be fruitful, or (Productive)

Adam was told to do three things In Genesis 2:15 which are applicable for us today if we want to prosper financially. Those three things are to tend, guard, and keep.

> Adam was told to **tend** the garden. To tend means to act, to move in a particular direction, to take care of your needs.

It also means a characteristic, to act and cultivate with character. God was telling Adam to respond to the needs of the garden with care. Adam was given the responsibility of feeding God's Creation. Animals before sin entered the earth ate from the same source as Adam. Financially speaking, we must handle earned income with care, with character, and move in the direction of spending it the way God designed. By giving to Him 10% to support the work of the kingdom and He blesses the 90% to take care of your earthly needs. Our families depend on our income to survive like the animals and Adam's family depended on his stewardship of the garden to eat and survive in a healthy way.

> **Guard**: In the Hebrew text the word for guard is Tab bah, it means to cook or prepare. Secondly it carries the meaning of a soldier or executioner assigned to protect. In regards to the garden, it would mean to pick the crops, prepare the food to feed your family by cooking it, and then give it to them for their nourishment and health. God prepared the garden of Eden for Adam. All he had to do was come receive what God had in store for him, and then take it back to his family and release the blessings from heaven to benefit them in the earth on a daily basis. This same principle was employed by the Lord in the Exodus story as God sent down manna from heaven to feed the children of Israel.

Therefore, our Father is teaching us to guard the method that God uses to sustain life for His children. ***Come, receive, release.***

- ➢ ***Keep***: The Hebrew word is Shaw mar it means to watch over, and to preserve. When it comes to money, we need to watch how we spend it, how we invest it, how we save it, and how we give it. Preserve means to save and not waste.

Let's put this all together. Ecclesiastes 10:19 says this: "A feast is for laughter, wine makes merry, and money answers everything." The word of God is telling us that money cures and solves all earthly needs and non-spiritual problems. Therefore, let us tend and be inclined to respond to life's needs with actions that are joined with God's in the area of prosperity. Guard prepare to be obedient to the natural process of the word which is both spirit and life. (John 6:63) It is not wise to go against the Lord's plan for money. Example: In a garden you must plant to reap. You must take care of the seed, (your income). You must cultivate the seed, to create multiple streams of income. One apple seed produces multiple apples from the tree. This is God's design by principle. You must do everything possible to keep weeds out of the garden. Weeds (the snares of the world) hinders the growth of what the Lord has designed to bless you with. Reserve the harvest. Extra money does not mean run and spend it. Extra money is for your future needs. Today's abundance is tomorrow's comfort.

CHAPTER TWENTY-FIVE

THE MINDSET FOR SUCCESS

My melanin brothers and sisters please hear this. You control the size of your harvest. You control the amount of money that God releases into your hand. You are blessed according to the level of trust that you extend toward God with your giving. For this reason, the Lord said that some receive 30-fold, 60-fold, or 100-fold. (Matthew 13:8) Why doesn't everyone receive the same? Let us look at it this way. God gives you 100 acres of land. One person uses half of the field. Another uses 30% of the field, while yet another, uses the entire field spending every dime that he has in seed.

One invested his all, while the other two had a different mindset, they kept money they could have used on seed in case it is a future drought, famine, a bad storm, frost or a bad year for crops. Each person reaped according to what they trusted God to return. God brings the rain, the sunshine, and the essentials that is within the earth to birth the seed. Corinthians 9:6 tells us that if you trust God sparingly, he can only return what you gave.

However, if you sow generously so you can help more people with your giving, and support the work of God more effectively, then God will return to you great increase. Mark 10: 28-31 gives us this powerful revelation.

"Assuredly, I say to you, there is no one who has left house or brothers or sisters or father or mother or wife or children or lands, for my sake and the gospel's who shall not receive one hundred-fold now in this time."

Jesus is telling us that if we put Him first before all other relationships and be obedient to His word, we will receive one hundred-fold in this life. Seek ye first the kingdom and His righteousness and all these things (MATERIAL) will be added unto you. Adam never had to work or earn what the Lord gave him. He was blessed by right relationship with God. When he sinned and chose a different path, which was the route or way of life that Satan offered him. Adam lost his provision from God.

Adam lost the land of gold and the riches that were freely given. Afterwards, he had to labor in the world by the sweat of his brow to earn what he once had easy and sweat less victory over. Therefore, if we are to flourish God's way, as a race of people, we must have the mindset of truth that says there is nothing too hard for God. All things are possible with God. I am the righteousness of God.

I am the head and not the tail. I am above and not beneath. I am more than an overcomer, I am a conqueror. I am filled with the spirit of God; I have the gifts and fruits of the spirit. I am anointed to prosper. I am a king and a priest. I am a co-heir with Christ Jesus. I have authority in the earth according to the word of God. *See Matthew 6:11, Matthew 19:26, Jeremiah 32:27

God's part in supplying increase

Many times, in life we are faced with challenges and obstacles that leave us uncertain in what to do. Sometimes our experiences in life will aide us, or at least place us in the ballpark of solutions. However, as the old saying goes being close only counts in horseshoes and hand grenades. When it comes to how we live according to the kingdom of God it is imperative that we understand that God has a part, and we have a part. We must work together in a heaven and earth partnership if we want the best results possible.

As we continue to evaluate the will of God concerning money, let us gaze at His part in all of this. We have covered many ways how the Lord is in the equation. However, I would like to get a little more specific. God gives us three powerful and impactful promises in His word that guarantees financial increase.

> ➢ God promises that His word shall not come back void. Isaiah 55:10
> ➢ God will give seed to the sower. Luke 8:11
> ➢ God will rebuke the devourer. Malachi 3:11

Why are those three keys important?

Let's open this up. In Malachi 3:8-11 when God promises to open up the window of heaven and pour out a blessing more than you can handle if you bring the tithe into His storehouse, He is telling us how to get a harvest financially. The divine principle is this; you cannot make a financial withdrawal where you have not made a financial deposit.

Deuteronomy 28:8, Is a promise that is connected to Malachi 3:8 where God promises to command the blessing on your deposit. Therefore, when God says His word shall not come back void or empty, He is saying He will deliver as He promised. We have confidence in this because we know that God is not a man that He should lie nor the son of man that He should repent (change His mind or rethink) what He promised to give you.

The word of God is both life and a spiritual guide for us to follow and live from. Jesus said in John 6:63, "My words are both spirit and life." Therefore, God says if you are not sure of how to handle something, I will give you a word from heaven.

Please note * He said if you are a sower, do you plant the word into your life? Do you live by what He says? If so, the Lord will send you the word that will set you free from your current circumstances and deliver His promise.

Here is the good part. We know that our warfare is not carnal. Meaning, Satan will try to prevent your harvest. (i.e.) In a garden weeds will try to choke your crops so that they cannot bless your family with healthy food and heavenly provision. In much the same way Satan will try to take your seed. Therefore, in Malachi 3:11 God promises to rebuke the devourer! God is saying I will take care of Satan. Do your part and I will do my part. This ensures financial increase when you are obedient in your support of the kingdom through *tithes and offerings.*

CHAPTER TWENTY-SIX

THE WARFARE OF WEALTH

Money carries a spiritual purpose for the kingdom. Therefore, it has a spiritual enemy. We learned this from Malachi 3:11 where God promises to rebuke the devourer. For those who are not convinced that Satan is the devourer. Examine the following scripture.

"Be alert and of sober mind. Your enemy the devil prowls around like a roaring lion looking for someone to devour." (1 Peter 5:8)

How we view money is due to education. Disobedience in how we handle money that God has provided us with is due to our free will. Vision is the first thing that we as the children of God must have. Proverbs 29;18 states that where there is no vision the people perish.

The word for vision is Chazon. By definition it means divine communication from God through revelation from His word. Money is God's idea. In Genesis 2:11 God gave Adam (Adam means mankind) a land of gold. We know and have discussed in an earlier chapter that Jesus was also given gold to finance His stay in Egypt.

Gold is also symbolic of kingship and wealth. According to Revelations 1:6-8, we are a royal priesthood. Therefore, it is vastly important how we see money. God says in Deuteronomy 8:18 that He gives us money to **set up the covenant that He made with our ancestors.** God blessed Abraham to be a blessing to many nations (ethos) meaning people. Money is to do the work of God in the earth.

Now that we understand what it is; for how do we carry it out?

Strategy is the second process. Webster's definition for strategy is a careful plan or method for achieving a particular goal. So, the goal is to do what? To set up God's plan on earth.

Always remember, increase of finances are never for selfish reasons. I have discovered a powerful scripture which gives great evidence about the strategy and mindset that I need to have about money. Let us examine and evaluate the following text.

"A good man shows favor and lends (Money), he will guide his affairs with discretion. Wealth and riches shall be in his house; and his righteousness endures forever." Psalms 112: 3, 5,)

The Hebrew word for strategy is EU KAIROS which means a time in need. *Divine inspiration of scripture is the strategic center of a Christians life.* Hebrew 4: 16 gives the children of God permission to approach the throne of God as a strategy to receive what we need in the earth. James 1:27 instructs us to support the widow, the fatherless, and the poor. When we think of the needs of others before our own, we take on the mindset of God blessing His Creation with grace, love, and provision. When we pour out, the Lord replenishes in abundance due to us having the heart of Christ willing to support people that we do not personally know but see their need.

To become successful in the issues of money we must have the spirit of expectancy. God will perform what He has promised. Therefore, let us discuss what hinders our growth financially besides disobedience to tithes and offering.

> ➢ End the mindset of not expecting money from God
> ➢ Deal with debt
> ➢ Cut poor stewardship

- ➢ Stop listening to the wrong voices about money
- ➢ Get educated Biblically… to lack finances is to be unlearned in God's plan for prosperity
- ➢ Always have a plan for your earned money
- ➢ No investments will hurt you eventually. Invest in something.

I pray that this chapter and teaching on finances has opened your eyes to the grave importance of financing the kingdom of God and being a present help to God's children. *"Surely, God is not mocked you will reap what you sow." Genesis 1:11 every seed reproduces of its own kind. And that includes money*

CHAPTER TWENTY-SEVEN

THE STORY OF TWO KINGS

As I envision America's inner warfare with racial inequality and social injustice, I can vividly see the unwavering faith in divinity that it took for our ancestors to face the horrors of broken humanity in the chains of slavery and the bondage of segregation.

As the shadow of death moved like a slithering serpent that threatened to silence the voices of morality, the zeal to overcome and rise above racism prevailed.

The courage of Martin Luther King Jr. challenged America's spirituality and her humanity as he stood in the nature of humility and bowed down to the power of faith and prayer. I can hear deep within my spirit the call of a king to a nation to repent and transform from the non- democratic and ungodly ways of her citizens. I can hear a rich and deep baritone voice of hope thundering from the mountain top..." In order for freedom to reign the horrid conditions of oppression and miscarriages of justice must change!" I truly believe that this transforming spirit that King hoped for is the spirit of love and the conviction of sin that must reach out and touch the hearts of men and women across this country.

I believe that love for one another is the only force that could both convict and eradicate the inhumane sin that plague America. The battle for human rights in the face of police brutality, the right to work and earn a living in the throes of COVID 19 during this economic depression of non- essential jobs is threatening our future.

A war in America for the right of collective dignity, common courtesy, human decency, and a pursuit of happiness regardless of one's personal beliefs is being waged in the streets of our cities.

If we are to change in this post Trump Era of: "Let's Make America Great Again!" mentality and the "Let's Take Back Our Country attitude, we must acknowledge equal value in one another, and alter our human conduct toward all of God's children. Today, we are bound by many social ills. Yet, the untwisting of a crooked disposition must derive from the intimacy of respect that can only birth through extending good will toward our neighbor.

Often, I ask myself where would the world be without the voice from the mountain top? Where would America be without the voice of reason that shook the consciousness of a nation steeped in the cruel treatment of segregation and hatred that echoed the wicked behaviorism of political tribalism? Our cannibalistic system of white supremacy feeds on the flesh of the poor, disenfranchised, marginalized, ostracized, and the urban dweller.

Our struggle with immorality, and the depth of dislike toward one another, is crippling our mobility to be better tomorrow. I stand in the shoes of hope, yet, before I can take another step into promise and progress, I reflect upon the lives of our ancestors and the verbal blueprint of Martin Luther King Jr. that both showed us and articulated a clear path to victory over what we face today. In the soul of my hope, I can hear the brave and uncompromising voice of demanding equality and human equity challenge the validity of separate but equal. This unyielding voice called upon the morality of all people to side and partner with love, and to socially distance itself from hatred and the unrighteousness of degradation toward people of color.

I can hear from the portals of history, a voice that feared not. A voice that stood strong and did not shrink under the daily death threats to both himself and his family. A king stood with his head held high resting upon a purpose larger than himself. A king heard the call of the Lord resonate in righteousness for man to do the mighty work of uniting the family of humanity.

Despite unparalleled evil and wickedness, the voice that alerted a nation was the language of diversity speaking through the articulation of beauty in both spirit and love. A king was exalted and raised up to welcome all of creation to the wedding feast, the great supper of the Lamb. We were called from the highways and byways of human indifference, selfishness, crime, mayhem, drug addiction and alcoholism. We were called from the desecration of denominational divide that separates the church of Jesus Christ.

We were called and welcomed to fellowship in freedom and to embrace with love while extending the blessings of economy prosperity.

Where would we be without the courage of a king? Have we answered the clarion call in 2021? As I reflect, who knew that if Martin Luther King Jr. would continue to preach the message of racial equality, the message of peace, the unbending embrace of love, and the unflinching power of the gospel that he would become a martyr and lay down his life so that negroes would one day become free from segregation and the horrors of extreme racism and discrimination?

King's purpose was greater than his fears even at the expense of leaving his wife and children alone in a cold and uncaring world to mourn as a widow, and to cry out as bastards. King marched on and never deterred from a call from the mountain top.

Moses knew about this mountain. Abraham knew about this mountain. Noah knew about this mountain. Elijah knew about this mountain. Jesus knew about this mountain. King did not stand on Mount Sinai and receive the ten commandments, though he did not take his son to be sacrificed on Mount Moriah, though he did not come to rest in an ark on Mount Ararat after the world was destroyed by the flood. No, King was not there on the

Mount of Transfiguration, and he was not there to preach the message on the sermon on the Mount.

Yet, Martin spoke from a high and lofty place. God himself exalted King, his life became a model of sacrifice that birthed change, not only for a race of dark-skinned people, whites were given an opportunity to free itself from the immorality of social and human injustice by agreeing with the voice of God that utters the words "Let us make man in our image." "Love one another as I have loved you"

King's life was a movement that was unceasing in purpose. As the day came when his speeches and sermons would stop. His voice in spirit did not cease even after the sniper's bullet left Martin Luther King Jr. slumped over in the throes of death. The powerful civil rights movement that was orchestrated by God elevated a people of color to cherish life's precious breath. King encouraged us to breathe freely and to move forward as dignified men, women, and children, fearing no evil as we unite and break the bondage of inhumanity and unrighteousness.

In 2020, moving into 2021 to achieve the motif of the National Association for the Advancement of Colored People we must acknowledge the *"Crisis and Challenges of Black America"* We must break the psychological chains of slavery. We must rise above the scarring of whips and the drowning of self-esteem. Our mighty nation did not perish with the sinking of slave ships.

Many bodies were thrown overboard, yet their plight and spirits hover above us today in the power of history and the infusion to fight with courage. We did not come from a culture of cowards. King's lofty, "I Had a Dream!" speech baptized a nation within the loving hope of a united human relations even in the midst of scorn, violence, and public lynching like what we have faced in this era in places like Sanford, FL., Minneapolis, MN., Louisville, KY., Chicago, and Baltimore. The voice of our Savior through a man of character, and of integrity spoke with a voice of new birth that was unmoving and courageous as he shouted globally for man to "Repent" His voice echoed loud and clear. "Division is not the will of God"

It's been 53 years since the assassination of King, and as a nation we are still experiencing racial divide, public lynching, economic disparities, social injustice, legal discrimination, and a high volume of illiteracy in our public-school system. We are still at war with civil unrest. If today, we do not know where to turn, let us remember the life and story of two kings.

Love is and has always been the template for acceptance and change. Love conquers all while soothing tension and pain with mercy and compassion. As a nation we can rise above the ignorance. We can rise above the voice that separates us during this unhealthy season by once again listening to the voice of reason.

Listen with me…I can hear the voice of the king of king's speaking from the mountain top. I can hear the God of the oppressed say; "Blessed are the poor in spirit for theirs is the kingdom of heaven. Blessed are those that mourn for they shall be comforted. Blessed are the merciful for they shall obtain mercy. Blessed are the peacekeepers for they shall be called the sons of God."

And so…in the face of police shootings, minorities seeking asylum, immigration reform, and gun control; in the face of political unrest, rumors of wars and broken social norms with the desecration of God's definition of marriage; in the face of terrorism and economic wars for survival; the tearing down of humanity through chemical warfare of mass destruction as drugs ravish our communities in addition to the sabotaging of family values, let us come as a nation to the terms of our greatest issue, which I believe is the rejection of Jesus Christ and the devaluation of one another.

Like a mighty rushing wind, I can hear the powerful voice of divinity speaking life into humanity. Let the nature of love reign in the hearts of one another and the unnatural occurrences of sin will organically cease as we once again reiterate the message from the march on Washington. Let us collectively strive for and achieve peace. Have we forgotten that with God all things are possible?

Have we forgotten the day when all races under heaven held hands in the spirit of unity and sung, "Free at last, Free at last, God almighty I am free at last!"

> *Discrimination, bigotry, and the ugly horrors of institutional racism must never again find a home to rest in! The evils of hatred must never again become welcome in our society. A new era has been born. A new national anthem has struck its chord with one accord in the hearts of America. We can be better, do better, and live better, because we are better that what history says we have become. In Christ we live and in Him we have the victory. Listen to His voice today.*

What a beautiful sound cascading down upon us from two voices crying out from the mountain top.

CHAPTER TWENTY-EIGHT

THE ULTIMATE GIFT

"Thanks be to God for His indescribable gift!"
(2 Corinthians 9:15)

I grew up in bondage and a servant to the streets of Detroit, Michigan, which quickly gave birth to self -fulfilling prophecies that said I would never amount to anything. I recall vividly the voices that said as a black man I could not do such and such in a white man's world. I heard it often said that I would die before the age of 21. I heard that I would end up in prison if I somehow survived the hood. No one spoke life into me. No one had hope in me, each time I walked out of my home I was faced with negativity. I was faced with the 'survival of the fittest.'

In the streets of Detroit this was life. I was faced with gangs, violence, and fighting the daily odds of hustling. Either I would get away or go to jail. At an early age I had the dog in heat syndrome which always breeds female temptations, and the ever-present dangers of drugs and alcohol.

Seemingly I was trapped in the ghetto with people dying all around me. I was trying to find reason amid unreasonable people and circumstances, which was like trying to find peace amid unpeaceful environments and hateful people. I was dealing with women trying to find love amid unloving people who was only after money. I was trying to find worth in a place that valued nothing or no one. I was lost for many years until I understood that my Creator, my Higher Power, had given me a gift. I realized that within my gift is my provision, which will provide me with everything that I need in life.

I came to realize that all gifts supply a need and a purpose.

No gift should be given that does not enhance a person's life and apply a deeper meaning to a relationship from the giver of the gift to who receives it, Gifts should reflect the level of involvement between the people exchanging them. They should be prioritized according to the relationship value. It would be wrong to give a man or woman an elaborate wedding ring when they have no plans of getting married. Yes, the ring is expensive, its beautiful and very thoughtful. However, the relationship is not on the level of meaning that the wedding ring suggest. Therefore, it sends the wrong message about where they are in the relationship. The gifts you were given by God reveals what type of relationship you have with Him. Your gifts reveal your value in the kingdom.

Today, I offer you the ultimate gift. I believe in order for us to meet the Crisis and Challenges of Black America, that we need to unwrap this gift and present it to one another. What is this gift?

- ➤ The gift of salvation: Restoring what has been broken beyond human repair (John 4: 10)
- ➤ Your gift will make room for you and bring you before kings and great men not because they are great but because you have been restored to your rightful place at the king of king's table (Proverbs 18: 16)
- ➤ Gifts of the spirit, the word of wisdom, word of knowledge, faith, miracles, prophecy, tongues, interpretation of tongues, discerning of spirits, and the gift of healing (1 Corinthians 12: 1-11)
- ➤ A gift is a precious stone to him who possess it, wheresoever it turns, whatever you apply your gift to it shall prosper (Proverbs 17:8)
- ➤ The greatest gift of all is love, for God is love (1 John 4:8)

Love is liberal and generous, but not wasteful. God's love is in control, but it is not controlling and manipulative.

His love is everlasting, but it is not conditional, nor does it grow cold. God's love leads and directs; but it is never misleading.

God's love corrects; but it never abuses. His love is intimate, but it is not lustful or giving in wrong relationships. God's love supplies; but it is not co-dependent. God's love supplies justice, but it is not bias.

My hope is that we will receive this gift and begin to heal as a people. I understand that we are all different, with a plethora of beliefs, customs, traditions, religions, and culture. However, if you were dying or sick and needed a kidney or a heart transplant. Would it matter who gave you the organ as a gift of life? Would it matter if the person were Muslim, Catholic, or a bum?

Would it matter if the person were white, black, or Asian? If you were on the brink of death and was granted another chance to live better, to do things differently, to be more productive, to give like you have never given before, and have the chance to be born again with the opportunity to love as you have never loved before. would you accept this blessing? Right now, is that moment God is offering you the gift to start over, to treat people better, to love with dedication, to give freely as it has been given unto you. God is allowing you to be effective in the lives of others, and to love yourself more by forming a closer relationship with Jesus. He has eternal life to give. Christ died so you can have it all: life, and life more abundantly.

Do not let this moment pass you by. Accept this gift and let your light so shine before men that God will be glorified.

CHAPTER TWENTY-NINE

THE VALLEY OF THE BONES

There is a powerful story that I would like to share with you that forever changed my life. I grew up hearing how happy people were in the church. I heard tales about people falling out in the floor through joy, and from being overwhelmed in the Spirit.

I heard about the thousands of people who flocked to mega churches that had unbelievably talented choirs, beautiful women, fancy cars, and sharp dressing members.

I heard about how family members got saved, and gave amazing testimonies where strangers acted like family, where love prevailed, and all type of miracles occurred. I desperately wanted to know this God. I did not want to just hear about Him, read about Him, or simply be a witness of His work in other people. I personally wanted to know Him for myself.

One night, I was really going through a lot and needing to hear from God, when I was given this dynamic story entitled the "Valley of the Bones." I was given this blessing about how God chose a nation of people as His own. He did not choose these people because they were great or mighty, nor due to being great in number; they were not warriors or hunters, God chose them because He had given His word to their ancestors, and because He loved them. (Dark skinned people)

The Hebrew and Egyptian people were called God's people above all the other cultures or ethnicities upon the earth. These blessed people of God had every possible advantage that one could enjoy in life. The Creator of heaven and earth performed miracles for His children. He defeated their enemies and fed them supernaturally.

God gave them their every request. He even gave them quail until they could not eat anymore. He quenched their thirst with water from a rock. God never left their side. We have that same promise today. Christ dwelt among them as a cloud by day and a fire by night. Every person God claimed as His own remained in perfect health and prosperity. In due season the Lord spoke directly to His servant Moses and gave His children the holy laws to govern their lives and to cover them in divine protection against all nations.

Yet, this blessed, and highly favored nation of people after all that God had done for them, like some of us today rebelled against the Lord year after year until they found themselves in a crisis.

The children of Israel became a species that was in danger of being extinct. God's children found themselves faced with warring against nations with large numbers, and against men of great strength, who were highly trained in warfare. These mighty kingdoms of men had the power to enslave entire countries of people. Yet, even during the rebellion, God called these stiff- necked people His sons. (Exodus 4: 22,23)

We can always trace the hand of God in our lives if we just honestly reflect on our past. Even though God had parted the Red Sea and had destroyed His children's enemies, even though He had performed many signs and wonders by defeating the sorcerers, soothsayers, and magicians, even though God shook the mountains and rained lightening from heaven; when God's children became faced with the giants in the land, they saw themselves as grasshoppers. They did not believe that they could defeat their enemies and take the promise land as the Lord had told them.

The children of Israel were afraid even though the Lord was on their side. How many of us today feel the same way? the church was carnal minded. How many land fields and obstacles in our lives are due to the battlefield of the mind? This poignant narrative that I am sharing with you is a powerful reality that is found in the sacred text of (Ezekiel 37:1-14)

> *Principle thought: Brother's and sister's, if someone is overtaken in any wrongdoing, you who are spiritual, restore such a* person *with a gentle spirit.*
> *(Galatians 6:1-2)*

The valley of the bones is a major crisis that depicts the condition of the African here upon the shores of America.

As I studied this narrative, I noticed that the prophet Ezekiel was not allowed to go into a critical situation of a deeply wounded and sick people through his sensual nature, or his five senses.

"If we look to be effective, we cannot truly reach people, when we come into the situation trying to deal with their issues in our own power."

In this age of social media, we are listening to too many voices. Everybody is not and cannot be counselors. God gives us this caveat for a reason. "Walk not in the counsel of the ungodly"

The Lord speaks to people and through people. Only the Spirit of God can speak perfectly into your situation. If a person goes into a trying situation that could present detrimental ramifications without being led by the Holy Spirit, attempt to deal with human brokenness on their own, often that person's own opinion and personal feelings about what you have done will sabotage or block the purpose of God's work.

If someone dealing with sin goes to the wrong person for counsel, often, that person will exalt themselves with a holier than thou attitude. Sadly, we as a people in many cases think that our personal sin is different than the "big" sin that other people do. We are often quick to judge, condemn, and crucify a person even though we have plenty of dirt on ourselves, we fail to see ourselves as being muddy.

God has said that none is good, and all have fallen short of His glory and standard of holiness. Ezekiel is no different than me or you. For this reason of human frailty God took the prophet and carried him, and strategically placed him in a spiritual position where God had prepared for him to be the most effective.

As we study the story of the valley of the bones you will discover that God sat the prophet amid a broken people. Ezekiel was not allowed to walk through, or around the broken people, or he would miss key issues and overlook certain things. He had to go in the midst of them and mingle with them, He had to notice their clothes, smell their odor, see what they eat, listen to how they talked to one another, and see what they value and dishonor.

Ezekiel needed to get in the trenches of life with them. It is hard for people to help you if they have no empathy. It is important that we picture this parable. Imagine the scene: You have a depiction of a valley of very dry bones. The terminology very dry bones give us the description of something that has become brittle, without nutrition, strength, and bone marrow.

If brittle and dry bones are stepped on, trampled over, or if they are driven any further into the dirt of left abandoned in this condition any longer, these brittle bones would become damaged beyond repair, due to the crushing of that structure. If you place pressure on these bones they would break, crumble, and return to dust. These bones are (symbolic of sinful people) they are dry, (due to an absence of Spiritual substance) they are lacking in godlike essentials. The marrow (Holy Spirit) or what gives the bones vitality is missing. Notice that the bones scattered throughout the valley still have their shape and form. This vivid picture that God chose to use as an illustration of his children is vitally important. (Beware of those in the form of godliness) For this valley (territory) to be full of dry bones (sinful people) God is showing us that whatever once was (purity in the church), i.e. their spirituality, and mindset have been eroded for a long time. Picture this earthly truth that tells us such a powerful spiritual fact. Think of this narrative depicting a young group of men who became trapped in the desert, and every one of them died. In order to fully grasp this picture, you would have to understand the stages of what a dead body goes through once a person has passed away.

➢ The smell of a dead body happens
➢ The flesh that was upon the body decays, rots, and eventually falls off the bones
➢ The hair then leaves the body

In time the bodies lying in the valley would lose its clothes, shoes, hats, until nothing will be left to identify the culture, age, sex, or origin of ethnicity of these bones (people).

All you would eventually see would be the very dry brittle bones that have been bleached by the sun (eroded by a sinful lifestyle).

As we evaluate this process think about how many years it would take for a living person to die and then become nothing but dry brittle bones as the only reminder that this was once a human life.

An amazing thing happens in this narrative. God asked Ezekiel, "do you think that these bones (people) can live?"

Please note* Ezekiel was in the spirit of the Lord. He was not allowed to view God's people with his five senses or in the flesh. Why is this important? The carnal mind is death, it cannot discern the things of the spirit. So, when Ezekiel was asked, do you think these bones can live, the prophet did not judge God's people for being in darkness. Why not When It is clear that the people were deep into sin? Ezekiel was in the spirit of the Lord. (He was seeing them the way Jesus sees us) He was not sent to condemn, but to lead them into the light of salvation by speaking a word over their lives.

In the answer to God's question Ezekiel said: "Only you know, God." Therefore, as followers of Christ, we should never condemn people no matter what they have done.

Today, people could be a murderer like Moses, Saul, or David, yet, these same men became the deliverer Moses, Apostle Paul, and King David a man after God's own heart.

"Every unsaved person is one word away from salvation"

Ezekiel's answer of "only you know, God," blessed me. It assures me that no one can know the purpose of why a person was created which gives me hope that my entire family will be saved before they leave this earth. I have hope for this perishing world because Jesus is still able to be found. Therefore, as we look at the world, the question looms large for us all. Can these bones live? can those who have been in addiction for years live? Can those in the street hustling, gambling, robbing, stealing, cheating, live? Can those who practice false religion live? Those who have been divorced multiple times, can they live?

As we study this story in Ezekiel chapter 37, we immediately see that God's love covers a multitude of sin.

God covers us in many ways…praise the Lord, and one of those way is that He does not allow everybody to see your current condition or else they would judge you, turn on you, gossip about you, or stop being your friend. That is why spiritual discernment is so vitally important. Often, these same types of judgmental people will not speak life over you, but death.

These are the folks who will say you will never amount to anything. You will be like such and such. You will be dead by the age of so and so. However, what people may think about you, does not matter. Ezekiel said, "only you know, God." And so…my life, your life, or the life of someone that you are praying for can take a turn for the better, like a person lying in their sick bed, being healed, or recovering in a certain period of time.

Let us examine what happens after God asked the prophet about the sinful condition of the church. God commands Ezekiel to prophesy over the situation that His children are in.

To prophesy means to foretell by divine inspiration. To speak a thing with spiritual authority and power and the spoken word happens at once in the earth. Therefore, God is saying speak a word that I have given you that will change my children's course of life and realign them to my purpose and will for them.

Therefore, what we say to people is spiritually important.

Word's primary purpose are not for language, or the interpersonal communication between two people.

The primary purpose of the word is to release power! This power speaks of our heavenly language through how we communicate faith.

Jesus gave us this revelation when He said that by faith you can say unto this mountain be ye removed, and it shall be cast into the sea. Notice that He did not say pray about the mountain being removed, He said speak to the mountain.

Let us examine a few more incidents in the Bible that articulates this point. When God was creating the world, He said, "let there be light," and it was. God says that the power of life and death is on the tongue. Jesus says in John 6:63 that the words that I speak are both spirit and life. Therefore, our words release power that affects change ordained from heaven.

CHAPTER THIRTY

RESTORATION

As we return to this story of the valley of the bones, this fascinating epic about the spiritual condition of the church. We pick up where God tells Ezekiel to speak a word over His people. (Ezekiel 37:11)

God said unto Ezekiel, "Son of man these bones are the whole house of Israel. Behold, they say, our bones are dry and our hope is lost, we are cut off from our parts."

How many of us today, feel this way, cut off? COVID 19 is killing people all around us. Unemployment is at a record high, homes are being foreclosed upon, hospitals are filled to capacity, and drug overdoses and suicides are ravishing our youth across America. Race riots, and a trying political transition that has further divided this country is taking place. At every turn, as a people we are faced with disfunction, trials, tribulation, and for many, a dismal future.

Many people who were once in the church have lost faith and no longer attend church. Sadly, God is a myth to people all around us today, either through rejecting Christ as the Messiah, or through denying there is a God that is in control over us all. The church feels cut off from Christ, the Messiah, the Savior.

One of the major obstacles that black people still face in 2021 is the misconception about Jesus and who He really is. The first hurdle is the belief that Jesus was blond, blue eyed and a part of the historical process of African slavery.

Secondly, is the belief that Christianity is a religion that controls through laws meant for Jewish people. Thirdly, is the disbelief of the resurrection of Christ and His deity.

To clarify this mythological belief of some black people, the Bible never justifies slavery. God foretells slavery, not to promote it, but to speak of a consequence of a culture of people due to rebellion against the holiness of God, and their choice to follow ungodly kings. In Matthew 25:41 the word says that hell was created for Satan and his angels, not for man. Yet, billions will go to this place of eternal separation from God. Not because God willed it, but because man choose to reject His plan of salvation. God wishes that none should perish. Death is against God's plan of eternal life for His children. Christ came to set the captives free not enslave us! In the Bible when God says obey your masters or those in authority over you, Once again, He is not promoting nor condoning slavery. God is teaching us that a prudent mentality is what we should have in a dire situation. God is saying due to being in slavery, or in any situation where other people's decisions dictate the outcome of our life, it would be wise to show the person or people in control the love of God, in the hope that it would ward off evil and not provoke unfair treatment beyond our current position.

Our problem or the black problem with white Christianity is this: White's believe in manifest destiny. Their America first, and white exceptionalism, which is the white mentality that says to blacks "just be good, obey us, work hard, and you will go to heaven." While they in turn acquire all the wealth and vital resources of the earth. However, there is no such thing as white Christianity. Christ is a King of a kingdom. Those who follow Him are kings and priest. We are to live a life that is Christ like, in behaviorism, and effectiveness toward other people. Christ is not a religion, He is a spiritual movement through the force of life that imparts, impacts, and inspires us to love and provide.

Jesus was not European nor Caucasian. He does not teach a Jewish religion. Christ said that a Jew is one who is spiritual. Therefore, those who emulate Christ's spiritual purpose and movement upon the lives of others are God's image and likeness.

Let us examine this same problem that the church had in the Old Testament that blacks have today. Let us evaluate the children of Israel's words in the book of Ezekiel during the story of the "Valley of the Bones" when they said: "We are cut off, lost, and without hope" due to wrong thinking, and unbelief.

Understanding this detrimental mindset of His children, God commanded Ezekiel to speak a new word over their lives that will change their outlook, and their current situation by instilling into His children a new purpose, a fresh perspective, dignified hope, and the divine ability to prosper.

What we think of ourselves and the self-defeating language in which we articulate toward one another sets a course of certain behavior that mirrors a lifestyle of hopelessness, from a lack of faith and respect for our own culture and heritage.

Another important ingredient that is found in what God articulates is this.

Notice that when God spoke about the church, He did not say some of my children. He said the whole house of Israel. Therefore, all had fallen short of His measure of holiness. The Jews need Jesus, or they too are doomed for eternal destruction.

We as a race of people and as a church are many members but one body. We are the inheritance of the Lord. God is not finish with us today! Though the church was steeped in sin in the valley of the bones, God did not leave them nor forsake them. The Lord never ceased believing in His spiritual investment in His people whom He crowned kings and priest. (Revelation 1: 6-8)

The children of God in this story are acting like both a sheep without a shepherd, a dis-banned people without a savior, and a culture without a history of love and divine provision. Like bones that are described as brittle, and very dry without marrow (inner substance) the house of Israel is under nourished from a lack of connection with the Lord, and spiritually weak from a lack of inner faith. If these people during this trying time in their lives, are spoken harshly to, if their feelings are hurt, if these bones are driven any further into their detrimental living, they would not be able to recover, repent, and become restored. I believe if the house of Israel is overlooked any longer, they would never receive the help they need. God will never allow us to go through more than we can bare.

Deep depression, and discouragement is often the fatal ingredients of becoming suicidal.

I believe as black folks we are in that same position today. Praise the Lord, God has a season for all things. Even God's redeeming quality has an end date before the Lord returns to judge and rid the earth of all sin. In Ecclesiastes 3:11 the word says that" God will make all things beautiful in time."

People of God who are frustrated with their lives, discouraged, or who may even describe themselves as non-religious; whatever title we give ourselves, please consider this truth: The church of that time was in such deep sin, or in such a terrible spiritual place for so long, that God gives us a vivid picture that portrayed them like a dead man, putrid, stinking, rotten, decayed, and past any medical help.

If God would have allowed men to judge His children, they would condemn them, just like many of us has been written off at some point in our lives. I know I was. Therefore, God had Ezekiel speak a word of hope, love, and life over a group of people who collectively thought that because they had sinned for so long that they were beyond redemption. Mentally they thought they were doomed for hell and permanent separation from their spiritual Father.

However, is there anything too hard for God? The Lord is teaching us an invaluable lesson here in how to deal with things in our lives. We can call a thing that is not as though it were.

As people of God it would be wise to give voice to the solution instead of mumbling about the problem.

In (Ezekiel 11:6) God says: "I will lay sinews upon you and I will bring flesh upon you and cover you with skin, and put breath in you, and you shall live and you shall know that I am the Lord!"

The crisis of many black men and women is a sense of hopelessness. We do not feel that there's justice for us in the courtroom. We do not feel that we are afforded proper equity in the workplace through financial earnings and job advancement opportunities. As minorities we are filled with trepidation even concerning things of God. We view marriage as something with no longevity or sanctity within the bond. For this reason, people across the globe have prenuptial agreements, and the old ball and chain mentality believing that relationships are restrictive and confines you from achieving fun and pleasure.

Couples who are financially successful live within fear that they will be taken to the cleaners if things go wrong. We as a nation of people are weary and restless in what we see as the white man's world. We do not believe that American history is African history. We built this country!

You cannot tell the American narrative and not include the vast contribution, productivity, and importance of the African descent here upon the shores of this country. However, there is a reason for our myopic pathologies.

After the ceasing of the whip blacks were still severely beaten by segregation, life in ghetto slums, the great depression, and hung by daily racism as an institution of bigotry that systemically placed blacks in the valley of the bones.

We have been discriminated upon for so long, mistreated so long, ignored, discredited, and poor for so long that we feel cut off from the rest of society and God's blessed people.

CHAPTER THIRTY-ONE

THE MEPHIBOSHETH FACTOR

There is a story in the Bible about a man by the name of Mephibosheth who was the grandson of King Saul. Mephibosheth had a valley of the bone experience. Due to the death of his father Johnathon and his grandfather Saul the young child was next in line to be king.

However, upon hearing the news of Mephibosheth's father and grandfather's death; the live-in babysitter who was entrusted with the care of the young child, panicked, and dropped the baby when he was five years of age.

The dropped child became lame and crippled at the feet. Many years later, when Kind David looked to restore all the blessings of the kingdom to the rightful heir of King Saul and sent for Mephibosheth, the lame man crippled at the feet, felt unworthy to receive the wealth and inheritance due to his physical condition, juxtaposed to his rightful spiritual position in Christ Jesus within the kingdom.

Proverbs 29:18 says where there is no vision. (Divine revelation from the word) the people perish. We must be able to see ourselves as God sees us. Mephibosheth was myopic toward his value in God. When he was summoned by the king to receive his wealth, this is what he said: "O- dead dog that I am, what do you want with me?"

"The hate that produced the hate"

Malcolm X

As African American men we often see ourselves as inferior, and unable to compete with our white counterparts.

Historically, we have been crippled by and dropped by those who were in authority to watch over us. We have been lied to by our teachers about the history of who we really are. In 2021 we are also in a crisis due to a sexual revolution that have buried our great minds in pornographic filth and verbal garbage through actions of negativity, because we believe that there's no place for us in the kingdom of God. However, God says in the valley of the bones I will open your graves (your dead mentality) and you shall come out of your graves (inferior thinking) and I shall put my Spirit in you and you shall live… now that you think differently about yourselves.

"Your actions are a direct result of how you think"
Pastor T.L. Hughes

"The very nature of mental slavery creates an illusion that we are free. This is the underlying shell that the Americans and African-Americans need to break out from."

Dr. Na'im Akbar

Breaking the chains of psychological slavery

This is our racial challenge in the valley of the bones. In the book of Ephesians 2:12 it reads: "At that time ye were without Christ, being aliens from the common wealth of Israel, and strangers from the covenants of promise having no hope and without God in this world. And He might reconcile both Jews and Gentiles unto God one body by the cross having slain the enmity thereby."

The challenge of the black race is to get up! To rise from the valley of the bones with a new spirit as a new nation unto God. We need to rethink who we are. We are not defeated; we are mighty soldiers and a royal nation of people. We are inventors, chieftains, prophets, kings and priest, mathematicians, lawyers, doctors, astronauts, engineers, journalist, firefighters, five-star general's, writers, pastors, movie stars, phenomenal athletes, musicians and rappers of unparalleled skills. We are many things that we have forgotten and can become once more. Have we forgotten that we have built civilizations, colleges, libraries, and great monuments in tribute to our greatness? People of melanin and Nubian culture: together, we have the victory! Do not allow your current condition to intimidate you and to defeat you. We are more than overcomers but conquerors through Christ Jesus.

CHAPTER THIRTY-TWO

PROTECT HER

"The least protected person on the planet is the black woman"

Malcolm X

Genesis 5:2 The word says: "And God created them male and female, and He called their name Adam."

This truth is so imperative. God sees man and woman as one person. They both are God's purpose, and vision for family. In marriage, God says," the two shall become one" (whole) A married couple is God's expression of humanity in the earth that reflects His holiness from heaven. Women are not inferior nor second class. The woman came from the inner spiritual source of man. Therefore, if a man does not understand the woman it is because he does not understand himself and who he is in God.

A woman is equipped and designed to give birth to what the man deposits within her genius, within her virile mentality, within her fruitful soul, within her nurturing heart, within her majestic spirit, and within her life- giving womb of sanctity. Men must protect the woman by keeping her mind safe from thoughts of insecurities and envisioning unfaithfulness due to his injurious behavior. We must be men of integrity and faithfulness. We must be dedicated to the vows and promises that we make to our spouses and significant others.

We must protect her heart by being non-abusive verbally, physically, and financially.

Men can be abusive financially when they withhold earnings, provision, child support, health care, and quality housing from their mates due to selfishness and buying things for "I and not we".

Men must protect her, his divine gift from other women. This is achieved by disallowing other women to even think that you will stray and cheat. Men, it is wise not to make your spouse or significant other need to defend your actions of flirtatiousness, crossing boundaries, and closeness to other women.

My wife is a feminine treasure that is both precious and priceless. She is a queen and the soul within my spirit.

She is my trust of love and the faith in my tomorrow, by being a blessing of human treatment. In all ways I understand that God has equipped me to protect her in every way that He does. We are kings and queens in God's kingdom. Yes, we are His crowned creation. However, we all have crowns that are both displayed with jewels and cracks. Because of those cracks, flaws, or defects, I cannot love my wife the way she is entitled to be adored by her creative purpose. I often tell people this. It's God loving my wife through me and its God loving me through my wife.

When we follow His word for how we are to care for one another then His loving spirit will reign supreme in our lives. The future that we see will be a result of who our beautiful black sisters give birth to. Therefore, the key is what type of men she copulates with. For this reason, Christ said; "Be ye not unequally yoked with unbelievers." Which is God saying; "Don't give your body, heart, mind, and soul to a person who is not connected and guided by my love and who I am in divine character."

CHAPTER THIRTY-THREE

HAVE YOU FORGOTTEN

Black man…black woman…how do you see me?

Please explain. If how you see me is in any way other than how you view yourself, how are we connected?

Are your struggles akin to mine, or are yours different, though we are both black men and women?

The affluent, are you apart from those in absolute poverty? Does materialism define your ethnicity, or does money pay for your soul and pave the way for your disconnectedness from those who are less fortunate than you?

Do deceitful riches suggest that personal wealth makes you exclusive from the masses of impoverished people of color?

Do you believe that a tailored suit or an expensive dress will cover your conscience and unrighteousness? How have you forgotten that the pregnant teenage child plays with your daughter?

Don't you remember that the young man who got shot sits next to your son in school. Have you forgotten that they are teammates in both football and basketball?

I know you frown upon crime and have moved out of the hood, but the father of three who was sentenced to life in prison, once dated your daughter and ate dinner in your home.

Yet, you act as if you do not know him, and cannot see his need for love and forgiveness.

I know the latest news was startling to most people when they heard that the local pastor was caught in a scandal. I know that many has disowned him, and many others after their fall from grace. Have you forgotten that the same pastor counseled you in your marriage, baptized your children, and buried your mother?

The homes that are today dilapidated and run down in slum neighborhoods, you once lived there.

> Yet, today, you drive past those same areas as if those
> people still living there does not matter.

The schools that have been closed housed your graduation and provided you with the education to earn the money you make at this moment. How have you forgotten? Do you dare believe that the sister with an afro is different from you because you have a weave that gives you an appearance of another culture? Do you dare believe that because you married outside of your ethnicity that those of your ethos is inferior to you, and that these negros are no longer worthy of your presence, and not good enough for your love and investment in humanity?

How have you forgotten where you are, where you have come from, and who you are? Is there no cause or reason that God made you black? How then, can you recreate what the Creator has created by sex changes and bleached skin?

My brothers and sisters around the world, I greet you as kin. I salute you for who you are in your uniqueness and I love you despite any reason that would suggest that I should not love you.

He without sin cast the first stone. As a culture I will never fear you, shun you, disown you, or hurt you. I say this because I dare not forget that we are one in the same. Yet, we have different experiences, lessons, and results from making different or difficult choices. We are family, either in sibling rivalry, or in close knit union. Whenever negative things happen, as an aggregate of people, we will either overcome them or become trapped by them. Black men and women, when you look at me, you are looking at yourself. We were all created in God's image and likeness or have you forgotten?

We face the same crisis and challenges of Black America. This is what slave conditioning looks like. (True story) A white woman commits a violent crime against a black man from a domestic dispute where she received ten years for his murder. During the trial at its conclusion. A black man who is the victim's brother hugs the white woman, the black judge hugs her after sentencing, and the black bailiff fixes the white woman's hair after the verdict.

> *"I am afraid African Americans have contracted Stockholm syndrome in the sanctuary and if you don't believe me invert the narrative! Imagine that a black male officer breaks into a white female praise leader's apartment. Would a white judge hug him and would a white bailiff fix his hair? Nowhere did I find Mary the mother of Jesus asking to hug Pontius Pilate!"*
>
> *Dr. Jamal H. Bryant*

ACKNOWLEDGEMENTS

The following are the beautiful people whom I used throughout this grand narrative to aid me in my validation of the crisis and challenges that we face in Black America from the bedroom to the bank account.

Alyssa Mancao
Martin Luther King Jr
Stephen Hawking
Dr. R.A. Vernon
Mother Teresa
Nikki Giovanni
Otis Moss the third
Ellen G. White
Apostle Michael Scott
Dr. Lynn Richardson, Glenda Bridgeforth
Dr. Matthew Stevenson
Malcolm X
Dr. Naim Akbar
C.T. Vivian
Marcus Garvey, Dr. Jamal H. Bryant

Printed in the United States
by Baker & Taylor Publisher Services